The Art of Intentional Thinking:
Master Your Mindset. Control and Choose Your Thoughts. Create Mental Habits to Fulfill Your Potential.

By Peter Hollins,
Author and Researcher at
petehollins.com

Table of Contents

The Art of Intentional Thinking: Master Your Mindset. Control and Choose Your Thoughts. Create Mental Habits to Fulfill Your Potential. 3

Table of Contents 5

Chapter 1. Mind Over Matter.............7
    The Inner Voice..........................11
    Self-Fulfilling Prophecies 14
    The Power of Thoughts 23

Chapter 2. The Mindset of Agency and Control 31
    Fixed vs. Growth Mindset 34
    Adjust Your Locus of Control 43
    Self-Efficacy vs. Helplessness ...50

Chapter 3. The Mindset of Perseverance 63
    Turn the Obstacle Upside Down.........65
    A Long-Term View 77
    The 40% Rule 85

Chapter 4. The Mindset of Action......93
    Thinking vs. Doing 97
    Solution vs. Problem Mindset ..104

From Motivation to Action **110**

Chapter 5. The Mindset of *Belief* **119**
   Think Big 122
   Systems vs. Goals 130
   The Alter Ego 135

Chapter 6. The Mindset of Gratitude . 149
   Create Perspective 152
   Positivity and Optimism 158

Chapter 7. The Mindset of Humility ... 171
   The Beginner's Mindset 174
   "I Know It All" vs. "What Don't I Know?" 178
   The Echo Chamber 181
   You're Never There: Perpetual Progress vs. Achievement 188

Chapter 8. The Mindset of the Present **195**
   Moving Beyond the Past 201
   Accepting an Uncertain Future 206
   How to Live in the Present 211

Summary Guide **221**

Chapter 1. Mind Over Matter

Courage versus fear. Comfort versus worry. Faith versus doubt. Confidence versus uncertainty.

These are battles fought every day—battles of *mindset*. And the arena in which they fight is contained within our brains. Whichever set of thoughts you allow to win will rule the day and your actions, and that is not a positive experience when disempowering thoughts win.

Indeed, for a few of us, the battles are one-sided. People who experience nearly constant success (or *think* they do) may be more able to disregard the negative or naysaying sides in the clash. Others who face mounting, daily struggles through an extended amount of time don't trust the positive voices.

We may perceive our mindsets as things we can't change or affect. We envision them as products of an external environment, circumstances, or history that are far bigger factors than we can proactively transform. The truth is that you have great capacity to modify your mindset. Goals and accomplishments that might seem impossible in an "entrenched" mindset can be attained much more practically than you may realize, just by reorganizing your way of thinking.

Is it easy to change your mindset? Of course it is! Except when it isn't.

Changing one's mindset is "easy" because there's no heavy lifting or manual effort. It's not a physical procedure that requires too much exertion. You could be doing it while sitting on a couch without anyone knowing—all you have to do is think something into existence and it becomes true. If you were to ask someone if they'd rather *think different thoughts* or work in a coal mine for 10 hours, it's not going to be a close decision.

But the ability to think a certain way on a consistent basis involves self-discipline and focus to the highest degree; changing a mindset is *hard* and can be frustrating because your effort won't directly translate into a different type of thought. You can always hit the gym harder, but thinking harder doesn't necessarily do anything. There is really no correlation between an input and an output.

Changing your mindset is especially tough if it involves countering what you've been taught all your life. A complete rewiring of your thoughts and mindsets is daunting at best but imperative to creating a life you feel happy to wake up to every day.

Like it or not, our mindset is our internal lens to the world around us. Our thoughts, opinions, beliefs, fears, and hopes get projected onto everything we see. We use those inner convictions to interpret everything that happens in the world and to us.

People who have attained the success you desire have all manipulated their mindsets in specific ways. You could argue that other factors—education, upbringing, luck, timing—produced their great achievements. It's easy to use those as an excuse for your lack of action, but the real-life evidence doesn't tend to support that. Is everyone rich simply lucky and rich to begin with and everyone poor simply lazy and apathetic?

Two children from the same middle-class family, who grew up in the same circumstances, can wind up in wildly different situations. One child with a positive mindset might turn out to be hardworking and wealthy. The other one could be consumed by a jealous mindset and a predisposition to failure and might wind up in a thankless job with low prospects.

The *only* difference between you and greatly successful people is in the mindset.

It's your view of the world, its challenges and rewards, and how you navigate through all of them.

The Inner Voice

Mindsets can be as varied as any given segment of the population. Here are just a few different mindsets you might possess to varying degrees:

- *Productive mindset.* Someone who is task-oriented and driven to complete what they're working on—and then move on to the next thing. They're a hammer, and everything looks like a nail. They are always in motion.

- *Creative mindset.* A person with unique abilities and inventive approaches who can solve problems in ways very few others can. They always seek unconventional methods to accomplish the same goal.

- *Confident mindset.* Someone who's happy with themselves and projects conviction, ability, and leadership. They naturally end up in charge and taking action first. They feel that anything is possible.

- *Dreamer mindset.* An individual who can see the big picture and is able to inspire others to take a broad and beneficial approach toward the future. They think big picture in lieu of details and procedures.

These mindsets affect and change someone's perception of the world. A productive mindset might see what needs to be done in their immediate environment, whereas the dreamer mindset might see its potential in an emotional or altruistic sense.

These are just some of the *good* mindsets. There are also mindsets for jealousy, anger, fear, greed, and the opposite of all of the mindsets above.

Self-talk—the commentary, criticism, and judgment we tell ourselves *about* ourselves—is one "channel" that your mindset tunes into, whether it's out loud or to yourself. Just think of it as your internal dialogue that never goes away, for better or worse. It narrates your life, but the perspective it narrates from is completely up to you. You can be your own biggest cheerleader or critic.

Each statement you think or say constructs your inner monument of self-belief, brick by brick. And we probably give a little more credence to negating self-talk since it's easier to believe we can't do something if we haven't yet tried. "I'm not smart enough to learn complicated math concepts," "I'm not physically gifted enough to run a 10-kilometer marathon," "I'm not attractive enough to have someone interested in me."

Another aspect of your inner voice is the *narrative*: the never-ending story that you tell over your entire life about who you are and what you're capable of. It explains what happens in your life and why you do certain things that you do. It often addresses "themes" or recurring events that occur in a lifespan. It usually isn't very accurate, especially if you tend to feel bad about yourself. Self-talk and the narrative have a chicken-and-egg relationship.

For instance, those with a victimized mindset claim that they were the patsies of people despite their best intentions. You claim you were fired from your job because your supervisor didn't care for your personality, but it might have been simply that their budget got a whopping cut and you had to be let go.

This isn't to say that your self-talk and narrative don't contain elements of truth or are completely unfounded. But it's important to check them with reality as much as possible. The more you can control your thoughts and inner voice, the more enabled you'll feel to make positive changes.

<u>Self-Fulfilling Prophecies</u>

The stories we tell ourselves through self-talk and narrative create a series of mental boundaries that can influence our lives dramatically. In fact, what we believe often comes true. This is called the *self-fulfilling prophecy*: something that becomes true because you've willed it into existence by telling yourself it exists. Your inner voice tells you a given outcome is so certain and absolute that, eventually, it becomes so. You almost give yourself no other option but for the prophecy to become real.

Technically, a self-fulfilling prophecy *could* be positive—but way more often, it's not. When a negative self-prediction manifests itself, that's the sign that your mindset needs improvement.

The phrase "self-fulfilling prophecy" was invented by American sociologist Robert K. Merton. Merton drafted the concept from an idea called the *Thomas theorem*, a hypothesis devised by fellow sociologists William and Dorothy Thomas in 1928: "If men define situations as real, they are real in their consequences." The theory declares that our subjective feelings or perceptions about a certain circumstance are more powerful than objective reality. To that end, real results are more often determined by interpretation than literal factors.

The idea behind the self-fulfilling prophecy is that a person's beliefs about a given situation affect how they behave. If one is absolutely certain of their understanding of the pending situation and its meaning, their external behavior about that situation will follow suit. That behavior, in turn, causes the emergent reality to unfold exactly to their expectations. This is called the *behavioral confirmation effect.*

A classic illustration on the self-fulfilling prophecy is *Oedipus Rex*, a Greek tragedy that gives a wildly different take on the concept of "family values." The characters in the play are all driven by a shared obsession with a dire prediction. One by one, each member of the family commits or endures horrifying consequences because they're convinced the prediction is inevitable.

Lauis, the king of Thebes, receives an oracle that informs him that one day his son will kill him and marry his wife (the son's mother). The king is so spooked and certain about this fortune that he abandons his son—Oedipus—and leaves him to die, figuring that will keep the whole sordid mess from happening.

But Oedipus survives and is raised by the king and queen of Corinth, who he naturally assumes are his real parents. Then *he* gets a prophecy that he's going to kill his father and marry his mom, so he takes off from Corinth to prevent that ugliness. Oedipus goes to Thebes, where he gets into a fight with a stranger near some crossroads and kills him. Guess who that stranger is? Yep, it's Lauis. But Oedipus doesn't know that he'd just killed his own father.

Oedipus, who's a little tortured by nature anyway, is eventually comforted by a woman named Jocasta, who thinks fortune-telling is kind of a sham and he shouldn't be so concerned about it. After all, once a prophet told *her* that her husband would be killed by his son, but instead he was killed by a highway robber near some crossroads. You probably know where that's going.

Oedipus and Jocasta get married. But then another prophet comes forward and tells her Oedipus's true lineage: she is his *real* mom, and he killed her husband, namely his real father, and by some hilarious miscalculations she is now married to her own son. I don't know how *you* react when you hear bad news, but Jocasta didn't take this information very well and proceeded to hang herself. Oedipus didn't go that far when he found out, but he did gouge out his eyes. It's twisted, it's convoluted; welcome to Greek tragedies.

So the self-fulfilling prophecy—that Oedipus would kill his father and marry his mother—wound up coming true, and the obsession that all in the family carried with them wound up driving them into the exact behaviors that would fulfill this prophecy.

One of the takeaways from *Oedipus Rex*, besides thinking twice about online psychic readings, is how the self-fulfilling prophecy had such a fatal sway over all the participants' lives. If Lauis weren't so convinced that his son was going to be a killer, he might have taken more rational measures instead of dumping him at the corner. He could have kept Oedipus and raised him with forethought and compassion.

Lauis could have brushed off all those stinking oracles and been father of the year. But by swearing to the wheezing fortuneteller's words and deciding there was nothing he could do about it, he saw the prophecy come true. Simple belief created reality.

Another angle of the self-fulfilling prophecy is when we latch onto a reality we want to believe, even when it's plainly obvious that it's untrue or detrimental. Let's consider another example that's not quite so squalid as Oedipus: the smartest horse in the world. A German animal trainer named Wilhelm von Osten had a horse he called "Clever Hans." Von Osten contended that Clever Hans could solve math problems, read, and spell like a reasonably intelligent child.

Clever Hans gave his answers to questions by stomping his hoof. If someone asked the horse what three plus four was, he'd stomp his hoof seven times. Similarly, when asked to spell something, Clever Hans would stomp his hoof according to the position of each letter in the alphabet (one stomp for A, two for B, three for C, and so on). This made von Osten sure that animals were just as intelligent as humans, just not able to sit at a desk. So he decided to turn his horse's talents into show business gold and took Clever Hans on the road as an exhibition.

Plenty of so-called experts thought von Osten had some sort of trick up his sleeve. But trial after trial they came to believe as he did: this was some kind of grand superhorse who understood math and language. Some even thought Clever Hans had the intellectual capacity of a healthy 14-year-old, which might not sound that magnificent but is pretty impressive for a horse.

One skeptic remained unmoved: Oskar Pfungst, a psychologist who ran a series of more controlled tests on Clever Hans. These tests were designed to get to the core of the horse's abilities and determine whether they were the result of great smarts or some other condition. Pfungst asked a lot more questions to remove the likelihood of "chance" results. He also mixed up Clever Hans's questioners, had them ask questions from different parts of the room, and told them to ask questions to which they did *not* know the answers. Additionally, he had Clever Hans blindfolded for some of the questions.

By running multiple iterations of the experiments, Pfungst discovered a few quirks about Clever Hans's abilities. He performed much better with certain questioners at a certain distance and had *much* more success when he wasn't blindfolded and when the questioners knew the answers beforehand.

Pfungst determined, much to von Osten's disappointment, that Clever Hans's responses were triggered by certain cues his questioners unwittingly displayed. For example, people would look down at the horse's hoof to count the taps; when Clever Hans reached the correct answer they might look up, which Hans had learned early on was a sign to stop stomping.

Instead of developing intellectual ability, Clever Hans was responding to very subtle shifts or changes in the movements of his askers—a remarkable feat in itself, but nowhere nearly as impressive (or financially lucrative) as a horse who knew math and language.

What does Clever Hans say about the self-fulfilling prophecy? That our beliefs play a huge part in our actions, which we take to make our expectations true. Von Osten came to a point of certainty about what was making Clever Hans run, and it informed his behavior and statements about the animal. Pfungst, on the other hand, couldn't be persuaded as to the horse's magical abilities—and by not getting caught up in the fantasy, he uncovered the truth and stopped Clever Hans's money train in its tracks.

Sometimes it's a persistent negative belief about ourselves that we can't shake, which ends up causing a negative outcome. Take someone who's had trouble finding a job. They're convinced they don't have anything to offer as an employee or at least believe what they have is easily replaceable. Perhaps they suffer from something called "imposter syndrome," in which one believes that they're conning everyone as to what they can do and it's just a matter of time before they get exposed.

This person can get as prepared as they possibly can for an interview—they can rehearse answering questions, look professional, arrive 15 minutes early, anything that gives them a heads-up. But the reality of their self-belief, or rather the lack of it, has a way of breaking through all that preparation. They manage to convince whoever's hiring them that they're not right for the job. The self-fulfilled prophecy comes true.

What difference would a higher self-belief have made? Well, a completely different prophecy would have been created.

The Power of Thoughts

Whatever is going on inside of our heads is *powerful*. But it's entirely conceivable to conjure up a *good* result through the power of thought—as we commonly call it, "mind over matter."

A research touchstone for this kind of phenomena is a highly cited paper by Henry

Beecher, which described the effects of fake medicine, or "placebos," to patients suffering from a certain kind of ailment. (The word "placebo" is a Latin word translating to "I shall please.") Most often these placebos took the form of a sugar pill that had no true physical effect on the patient, but sometimes they involved a "sympathetic" physical examination as well.

Beecher claimed that using the placebos resulted in a 30% improvement in the patients' health. They assumed that they were taking an action (or a pill) that would help their condition, and for many of them, that belief itself contributed to their recovery. Overlooking the trickery involved, this demonstrates a good deal about the power of suggestibility in creating a positive effect.

The placebo effect is, many believe, more useful to treat psychological conditions rather than physical ones. A recent experiment revealed that 60% of depression patients who received placebo treatment showed improved results over a waiting-list control group. This suggests to an even greater extent that the power of suggestion is a strong motivator, particularly in issues more connected with mental and emotional health.

Since the placebo effect draws from the usage of a "remedy" that isn't made to have a "literal" effect, many have doubts about its effectiveness. But the placebo effect is no hoax, and it's not the product of an accident, experimental irregularity, or partiality. It's a real outcome that works with the functionality of the brain. When the brain anticipates a certain result, that anticipation plays a heavy part in affecting how it all comes down. It's the self-fulfilling prophecy that mirrors what the brain would do if it were generating all the events it wanted to. Thoughts can affect the real world, even if it's not something that you intend.

Subtle shifts in mindset can affect more than expectations, demeanor, or attitude—in certain situations they can produce meaningful and measurable change. Harvard psychologist Ellen Langer ran an experiment to test that theory.

Langer collected a group of 84 hotel maids who were mostly overweight. Even though all topped their daily recommended total exercise in the course of their duties, 67% of them didn't think they were physically active. Langer theorized that the maids' perspective about their physical activity was hampering their ability to lose weight. In other words, whether or not they believed they were healthy made them so.

The maids were divided into two groups and measured. Langer praised one group that its level of daily physical activity was far more than what the surgeon general suggested. She said nothing to the other group.

One month later, Langer's research crew came back to the hotel to review the maids' progress. The half who received praise and full information on their exercise showed strong improvements in vital health factors: weight, systolic blood pressure, and waist-to-hip ratio. The group who received no information didn't show any meaningful changes at all.

Langer concluded that the maids' awareness of their physical activity served as an engine for their physical improvement and likely resulted in bettering their *mental* health as well. Langer's speculation was strengthened by the maids' managers saying they didn't notice any substantial changes to employees' routines.

With nothing more than new knowledge about their everyday physical activity, these maids achieved results that the others didn't. They didn't alter their daily routines, and they didn't take on any special programs. Just by having their thinking reset, they were able to make some relevant and healthy changes with tangible results.

This study shows how powerful an affirmative mindset can be, even when all other factors of one's life don't change. The maids were all taking reasonable steps already to maintain a healthy existence—but the addition of an affirmation to their already-existent mindset gave them a healthy, unexpected boost.

This is a startling example of just how much power the mind can have. Of course, you can't think yourself thin by saying "I'm physically fit!" while chowing down on cheese puffs and sitting in front of a television for 10 hours.

The power of positive thinking, self-fulfilling prophecy, and changing the mindset is real. It's not anti-science, new-age puffery, or wishful thinking. What the mind can do all by itself to push one to become a better person, scholar, practitioner, or even partner can be astonishing. And this book will go into proven ways that can change your mindset for life.

Takeaways:

- What is your mindset? It's how you see the world, yourself, and your place in the world. It's the overall lens you view everything through. It includes your self-talk, your internal voice, and the narrative or story you tell yourself *about* yourself. It's not technically hard to change because there is no physical activity involved, but it's hard because effort doesn't always correlate to results. Simply thinking different can be one of the toughest tasks in the world.

- Mindset has the power to shape your reality, as proven by the concept of the self-fulfilling prophecy. Famous instances of this include Oedipus and Clever Hans, a horse who appeared to be able to do arithmetic and read. This, along with the placebo effect, wherein a belief or expectation makes that belief or expectation exist, are stunning illustrations of how powerful your mind can be. It's not just positive thinking; it's thinking strategically about what you want and what you don't want. In a sense, your mindset should enable you to put mind over matter or simply overpower your circumstances through your beliefs alone.

Chapter 2. The Mindset of Agency and Control

With all the action, information, and activity that happens in our everyday lives, it's easy to believe that nobody truly has control over their own lives. Change is "forced" upon us and we've got no say in the matter. Achieving our dreams is more a matter of luck and external factors instead of working to get it. We are simply products of our circumstances and environments.

Right?

I once had a friend I'll call Ned. We briefly went to the same college after graduation. Ned had a great affection for movies and was kind of a walking film encyclopedia. He could cite the cast and crew of almost every major motion picture that came out in the 20th century. Although he had an enormous interest in acting, he was discouraged by a family who didn't believe it had any creative talents.

Ned was drawn to acting in school and signed up for drama class. Every year they'd put on two productions, a play and a musical, and everyone in the class was guaranteed some kind of part. Ned *never* got more than a line or two in a play, and in musicals they'd always put him in the background chorus. In fact, he never auditioned for major speaking parts the whole time he was there.

We got to know each other a little better when we enrolled in college, and I asked him why, with all his knowledge of cinema, he'd never pushed himself to learn more or gone for a bigger part. "My family is very practical," he said. "My parents thought there was no future in any kind of artistic activity, and they always told my sisters and I that we weren't genetically disposed to be talented in the arts." Drama class didn't help because there wasn't a lot of *instruction* going on—it was either auditions or rehearsals, pretty much all year round.

So imagine my surprise a few months later when Ned landed the lead part in a college production of *Who's Afraid of Virginia Woolf?* Did his high school drama teacher miss something that his college professor picked up on? "Nope," Ned told me. "It wasn't until high school was almost over that I started to feel that I *could* be good at acting. My dad felt bad that he might have discouraged me—he really didn't mean to—and that summer I actually took an acting class. I was surprised by how much of it was a process. I just thought the kids who got the big parts had natural talents I could never compete with. But it turns out they had to work at it, too. So I determined I'd just find out what the work was like and see if I could do it."

The mindset we discuss in this chapter is one of agency: you're not a powerless bystander in your own life. Ned had the ability to control his actions and future, and so do you—everything in your life is under your control; you just have to believe it first to put it in action. Change and control are possible, though not easy; outside events and external factors are only part of the equation. Your mindset can overcome all of them.

As hard as it is for us to believe that in times of distress and victimhood, it's an empowering truth that can see us to our greatest heights. To get yourself into a mindset shaped for controlling your own destiny, there are a few theoretical models that can help you focus on what kinds of thinking you might need to change.

Fixed vs. Growth Mindset

What we believe about ourselves and our abilities is a fundamental part of how much agency we feel we have. Some of us believe we can't change or evolve who we are, whereas others eagerly seek out new experiences, challenges, and education precisely to grow and develop. These opposing approaches are the "fixed" and "growth" mindsets. This is the first way that we determine whether or not we take agency in our lives.

The *fixed* mindset states that intelligence, talent, ability, and performance are all firmly determined from cradle to grave—they can't change or grow. You are what you are, and if you don't have something by now, you'll never have it—you never had it in you.

What's the purpose of trying if you don't think it's in you? The fixed mindset is quick to avoid challenges and even give up before a problem can be solved. It doesn't value effort; it views excessive work as "trying too hard" for little to no payoff. A single criticism can derail an entire project because the fixed mindset has already determined that what it currently has is all it's going to get. This is where Ned started because he felt that acting simply wasn't in the cards for him, and so he never took steps toward it.

The *growth* mindset is fundamentally different because it assumes change and growth are possible. Whatever you are right now is just a starting place from which to grow, improve, and develop. In this approach, nothing is impossible because it takes the position that learning and growth are almost always rewarded in some way. The possibility is there, and thus people seek opportunities out. Challenges and obstacles aren't avoided; they're dealt with and learned from.

Constructive criticism is welcome feedback digested in the spirit of helpfulness. The growth mindset is always evolving, always learning how to make things better, and always considering how to improve. This is what Ned skewed toward at the end of the story from earlier because he felt that acting was something he could develop and grow, even though he felt he was initially poor at it.

The growth mindset is what you'll find in people with higher levels of success. The differences between fixed and growth mindsets manifest in several ways, from a particular kind of action to variances in speech and messaging:

Fixed mindset	Growth mindset
Wants to appear smart or capable	Wants to learn and improve
Says "I don't have the right set of talents" or "I'm not naturally gifted"	Says "I can learn to develop more talents" or "If I learn this new skill, my capacity will increase"
Gives up when problems or barriers arise	Powers through roadblocks
Disregards feedback or construes criticism as negative	Welcomes constructive criticism
Says "I did the best I could"	Says "It's okay if I didn't get it all right in one shot—with gradual work and practice, I'll get better"
Resists leaving the	Pursues new

comfort zone	challenges

Let's take something as simple (yet ambitious) as learning a new language. The fixed mindset enters the endeavor with the expectation or hope that it will be easy to pick up. But a few lessons in, the fixed mindset might get impatient if it's not getting the pronunciations correct. It'll get frustrated and reach a certain plateau it doesn't believe it'll overcome.

It'll stop practicing and decide it's not worth the effort, thinking there's no point in continuing because it doesn't have "what it takes." It'll declare that it's just "terrible with languages" and move on to something that feels easier.

But a growth mindset would embrace the opportunity as a chance to expand itself. It'll complete each step in its lesson plan patiently, working slowly enough to understand and comprehend each part of its study. It knows effort and time is an integral part of its growth equation.

It won't stop at the first sign of failure, will keep practicing, and will seek out assistance wherever it can get it. It'll be eager to learn more complex phrases or concepts as it goes along and might even expand its studies by learning more about the culture of its language or even another language altogether. By adopting the growth mindset, you're exerting control and power over the circumstances in your life. No excuses.

Researcher Carol Dweck, who's spent her professional career investigating and championing the growth mindset, observed some of the shortfalls educators unwittingly displayed when dealing with their students that led them to a potentially "false" growth mindset.

In essence, the development of the *false growth mindset* boils down to the educators praising the students' *efforts* rather than their *process*. The growth mindset focuses on the deliberate execution and gradual understanding of concepts. In Dweck's observation, some teachers praised their kids with generalized platitudes like "good effort!" or "you can do anything you set your mind to!"

Someone with a genuine growth mindset gets more specific about their praise. Rather than applauding the person, they compliment their process. Instead of exalting who their students *are*, they commend what they *do*.

For example, a fixed mindset would say, "Gosh, you're really smart at math!" A growth mindset, on the other hand, would say, "I like how you worked on this problem by trying different approaches and how thoroughly you tried to solve the equation with these notes. You put a lot of work into this." A false growth mindset would simply say, "Great job for trying! Keep trying!"

Just saying the student is smart—which they very well may be—only reinforces their identity. Complimenting the work they put in strengthens their actions and gives them the reinforcement that change is possible through action and effort.

The instructors certainly didn't *intend* to cultivate the fixed mindset in their students, but speaking in such ambiguous praise doesn't take the step-by-step nature of the growth mindset into consideration. It may have given the students a false sense of progress or expectations, taking their mind off the very gradual experience of the growth mindset.

The primary realization is that the growth mindset is about learning, not generating. Leave the self-congratulations and look toward each next step purposefully. Acknowledging your own progress is important, but anticipating your next moves is a great way to keep you focused on your motivation to always learn and improve.

The growth mindset is obviously well suited to educational endeavors, but it works in many other areas. In business, a growth mindset allows you to seek new opportunities and areas in which you can improve. A businessperson is more enthusiastic about making contacts, understanding employees' roles, finding untapped markets or approaches, and projecting into the future if they feel that their efforts will have an impact.

Personal relationships and friendships also benefit from the growth mindset. A fixed mindset is always looking for the perfect partner, someone who checks off every trait on their list and will live with them happily ever after. But if they discover flaws in the other person—or themselves—they feel they're just part of who they are and they won't be able to change, whereas a growth mindset knows that all relationships take work and honest, active engagement with others. They know love isn't a magic potion that solves everything; it's a consistently developing process that matures and grows the more it's tended to.

Finally, be aware that it's almost impossible to be in growth mindset 100% of the time—you *will*, occasionally, find yourself rooted in a fixed mindset where you feel you've hit a wall or a ceiling. It happens. When it does, you might beat yourself up a little about it because that's what a fixed mindset does: it judges according to a final result or lack thereof. But spin off that critical voice by examining what you might have missed, diagnosing it, taking it into consideration, and trying again.

You don't have the time or pressure constraints in the growth mindset. You're here to learn. You'll get to your destination eventually, and by absorbing all you can about your process, it'll be better in the long run. So will you.

Adjust Your Locus of Control

I have a childhood friend that I don't think has ever taken responsibility for a day in his life. He still lives at home with his parents (at age 35), which by itself is fine, but he does so out of necessity and a career path that may have peaked four years ago. He was also placed on academic probation during college and subsequently flunked out the next semester. And he's about 20 pounds over what I might call a healthy weight for him.

You can be all of these things and still be a wonderful person—and he is. The problem with him is that he doesn't believe that any of his life circumstances are actually his fault, and that's what keeps him there.

He says they are out of his control, he's done all he can, and it doesn't matter if he tries—things always just "turn out badly." It's never his fault, he's not meant to succeed, and the cards are stacked against him.

He believes that what happens to him is entirely a result of external factors like fate, luck, people having it in for him, or just because "that's the way the world works sometimes." He's still living with his parents because the economy is terrible and jobs don't fall out of the sky. He's not going back to school because he's not lucky like other people who study subjects they really like and he doesn't learn well in traditional settings. And his weight? He doesn't exercise, he's got a thyroid problem, and he thinks diets are generally scams.

My friend has what is known as an external *locus of control*, which is part of a theory popularized by Julian Rotter in 1954 about how people view the *loci of control* in their lives.

A locus of control refers to where people feel control in their life resides—internally or externally. If you feel your life is controlled by outside influences that no amount of effort from you can change, you have an external locus of control. The external locus view decreases the amount of control you have down to almost zero. This is a mindset that is highly detrimental to the pursuit of success, happiness, and maximizing your potential.

When you don't feel that things are within your control, there is no logical way that you will take responsibility or fault for anything. Thus, you don't make any effort to improve yourself whatsoever—because in your mind, there is no correlation between your efforts and what happens! Why even bother if you are going to be subject to the whims of the world and other people?

External locus people focus on things that happened in the past. They focus on situations in which they really do not have a say. They focus on the lives of other people. They hope people will magically change or that situations will stop happening to them. They simply hope, wish, and pray that things will be different. This is someone who sits quietly in their room in the hopes that their comfort zone will suddenly burst or increase.

The time you invest worrying about things you have no voice or control over is wasted. You let the fiction that you are not in control of your life get the best of you. You throw yourself a pity party.

Let's compare that to someone with an internal locus of control. By contrast, a person with an internal locus of control believes that outcomes and successes are directly tied to their level of effort and work. And of course, if they fail, it's because they did not try hard enough. If the missing element is effort and action, then that's what will increase ten-fold.

Those with an internal locus of control feel they are impacting the world and making their mark on it, as opposed to just living in it or being subject to it. They are proactive about what they want because they know that's the only way it will come to them. As a result, they are very goal-oriented and focused because their actions have direct consequences, as do their inactions. They have the power to affect their lives on a daily basis.

Internal locus people don't accept a lack of success and are active to remedy it. External locus people passively accept whatever comes their way because they don't feel they can change it.

Here's an example to illustrate. Say that you keep getting passed up for a promotion by younger, less experienced coworkers. Understandably, this is irking, and this is where the divide of locus begins—the source of that annoyance.

An external locus person might suspect that there is a conspiracy brewing. He thinks, "My boss is an assh*le and has always hated me. In fact, he's threatened by me because I'm better at his job than he is. Besides, he's jealous of my wife." The external locus person blames factors out of their control and doesn't look inward. They choose to be a victim.

An internal locus person might start looking at their own actions and examining how they tie into their actual job performance. They will ask themselves, "Am I showing up to work on time? Putting in enough hours? Meeting minimum quality standards? Taking too long for lunch breaks or leaving early too frequently?" Their focus is on examining their own actions and not looking outward. This is choosing to be a victor.

If the latter scenario sounds more familiar to you, that's good news. You realize that your results are directly related to your actions. The results you crave? They are yours for the taking! It all begins and ends with your realization that when you focus on the things you *can* control, you can change your life.

If the former scenario sounds more familiar to you, that's not necessarily bad news. It's probably not intentional on your part. It means you need to adjust how you view your locus of control and acknowledge that your outcomes are indeed directly caused by your actions. Instead of worrying about things you can't control, recognize that channeling emotional and mental energy can be what changes your life. No excuses!

Ultimately, there is nothing fundamentally different about people with different loci of control. They experience the same events and hardships, but they simply perceive them differently. Successful people with internal loci of control take reality as it comes and impose their will on it. They do not blame other people and circumstances for what happens. They take responsibility and control.

They look at the world as a set of stimuli that they only need to respond to and take control over by using their will. They focus on what they can directly impact until their spheres of control continue to spread.

Self-Efficacy vs. Helplessness

Henry Ford famously said, "Whether you think you can, or you think you can't, you're right."

He was speaking to the matter of *self-efficacy*—the confidence we have in our ability to handle and execute in given situations. The mindset of feeling you actually *can* do something is a massive contribution to all efforts you undertake, even more than talent.

Self-efficacy is a nearly universal element in almost any success story. By nurturing belief and confidence in your abilities, you can start a chain reaction that funnels down through your efforts, understanding, and accomplishments. The more resolute one is that they *can* do something, the more likely the chances that they actually *will*. And the more they accomplish with this mindset, the more control and agency they have over their own fortune. If you assume, even brashly, that you can tackle a task, you'll try and succeed or try, fail, learn, and then succeed in the end again.

And again, this is a simple switch to flip mentally in deciding how you view the obstacles in your life.

The opposite of self-efficacy is helplessness, in which an individual perceives that they have no control over a given situation—and therefore no control over their own fate. Helplessness promotes a fatalistic outlook, which in turn makes one less willing to put energy into anything. They've already decided their goal is out of reach, so why put any effort into it? You might as well just curl up into a ball on the ground.

It's not always easy to build self-efficacy, but it's something we can pick up from several sources. Albert Bandura, the Stanford psychologist who first theorized about the self-efficacy mindset, identified four different means by which we can build a self-efficacious mindset.

Mastery experiences, or "just doing it." You've done it before, so you can do it again. With every successful completion of a task, project, or goal, we add and accumulate more self-efficacy and confidence in our abilities. It takes tenacity to power through the process and conquer the snags, but that's exactly the concrete evidence we need to feel good and reassure ourselves. Any extended time working on a particular skill or project—writing a book, completing an exercise routine, researching a report, making exotic cocktails—helps build the mastery mindset.

Vicarious experiences. As the name implies, these kinds of experiences come from observing those around us, especially people we've set up as role models for the kinds of accomplishments we want to make. By seeing others attain favorable outcomes from their efforts, we become encouraged that we can replicate their success ourselves. Using the examples in the last paragraph, those include your favorite author, a physical trainer, a seasoned journalist, and whoever the best bartender in your location is. *Monkey see, monkey do* is a surprisingly empowering way of thinking.

Verbal persuasion. People who we consider authority or mentor figures—parents, coaches, teachers, tutors, supervisors—play a huge part in developing self-belief, encouragement, and faith in our success. Their support and guidance make us more likely to stick with a given task and transcend obstacles. This could also include personal friends or associates on the same level who respect your enthusiasm and abilities. If someone that has the authority and experience to know otherwise believes in us, we will take it to heart.

Emotional and physiological states. How you're feeling—your overall mental state and how you feel at that particular moment—will naturally affect your level of self-efficacy, especially if you're feeling negatively.

It can be hard for someone suffering from depression to build confidence in their abilities, and states of panic or strain can be viewed as susceptibility to challenging situations. The happier we are, conversely, the more assured we are. We think about happy and successful outcomes and assume that things will go our way.

Negative emotions—the feeling of failure after not being able to finish a book, discouragement at your weight training progress—affect your mindset. But don't underestimate the power of positive emotions on your sense of self-efficacy: the relief of a completed research paper or the satisfaction of a fantastic cocktail with one of those little umbrellas in it.

Self-efficacy is a trait that can be bred and cultivated, and it helps us maintain control over ourselves. We develop self-efficacy by consistently working, watching, and learning from others, courting constructive feedback, and focusing on and celebrating success. After walking through the fire, we understand how we can impact the trajectory of our lives even when everything appears to be going south. Its opposite, helplessness, might be perceived as something that one just "gets," whether they're born with it or have it thrust upon them. But here's the surprising thing:

helplessness is something that's *also* learned.

In the 1960s, scientist Martin Seligman conducted experiments on dogs that were a variation on the famous classical conditioning trials conducted by Ivan Pavlov in the early 1900s. Pavlov "trained" his dogs to salivate at the ringing of a dinner bell, which to the canines obviously meant they were about to get fed. Seligman, on the other hand, tried to reverse the effect (in ways I personally think were a little cruel—but, well, *science*).

Rather than food, Seligman used a light to alert the dogs that they were about to receive minor electric shocks through the floor of their cages. His theory was that the sound of the bell would cause the dogs to escape over the wall and into the next cell.

At first, the dogs who were just introduced to the shocks for the first time did try to escape them at the flash of the light. But to his surprise, dogs who had been subjected to the trial multiple times did *not* try to escape when the light flashed. Instead, they stayed in the electric zone and braced themselves for the shock they were about to get.

Seligman's conclusions were astounding: over time, we are *conditioned* to respond to adverse circumstances or imminent misfortune by giving in—admitting helplessness. The dogs had "learned" that there was no way for them to avoid the shocks; they were going to keep happening whether they tried to escape them or not. So in the latter stages of the experiment, they just gave up and lay on the ground and did nothing. Humans do the same thing but in slightly more dignified ways.

The implications of this finding range from annoying to possibly tragic. A person who's belittled about his intelligence or learning may always figure that he'll never be able to learn math or science, so he doesn't even try. More grievously, victims of physical abuse may never try to escape their surroundings because they believe it would be fruitless to even try—things won't get better anyway.

So the mindsets of self-efficacy and helplessness are *both* conditions that are learnable and lead to polar opposite results. Self-efficacy increases one's motivation to work with confidence, take on new challenges, and navigate confidently through trials or negative situations that come up in life. It's vital to strive toward the self-efficacious mindset and to try to reverse the effects of the helplessness mindset as much as possible. Instead of giving in to feelings of futility, focus on what you can control and know that you have the power to shape your life.

For example, let's say you work at a company that's on the verge of making some budget cuts, which could very well mean layoffs. Nothing spreads terror through an organization like the prospect of impending unemployment. A person with the helpless mindset believes the entire process is out of their hands. Their destiny is controlled by an outside force, they were probably doomed from the outset, their morale is in the tank, and there's no point in wasting any effort.

The self-efficacious mindset, on the other hand, helps people work as diligently and as thoroughly as they can. They realize they can't control what will happen at a level they're not on. By working with as much pride and confidence as usual, they know that if they get laid off, it wasn't because they failed. They know that these challenges happen, and how they manage through these negative situations is what defines who they are. That kind of confidence could lead to a new situation more readily than they might expect (if, that is, you even get laid off in the first place).

The first step in changing your mindset is to understand that you have all the tools you need to make it happen and that the power's in our grasp.

There is another way to think about the difference between feeling self-efficacious and empowered versus feeling helpless: whether we imagine ourselves to be the main or supporting characters in our lives.

The main character is the focus of the story—they're the ones whose actions, feelings, and proclamations carry the most weight and whom we pay attention to the most. Supporting characters are essentially there to serve others. Even if they have a special skill or do something that *seems* heroic, ultimately they're only important in how they affect the main character. We don't fall into one role on purpose, but we can easily get caught in being a supporting character in our own lives.

Let's take a look at shadowy superhero Batman. You might be familiar with the fact that he has a butler named Alfred to attend to his needs and act as a confidant.

No matter how great a butler Alfred is, he's ultimately there to support Batman. He might flip a switch here and there and do something that *impacts* Batman, but it's only as a role player. Batman has to do the heavy lifting and save the world. All eyes are on him. When Batman's out saving the world, Alfred is contenting himself with a pot of tea. Maybe he's watching Batman on TV, but that's all: watching. Alfred doesn't have any control over what happens to him as a consequence of being Batman's employee. The plot is all about Batman, and because of that, he wields the power to change things. Which of the aforementioned people do you identify with more?

As the central character in your own story, you're in control of what happens and have the power to determine how the plot unfolds. I'm sure all this reads like very creative daydreaming. It is, and that's the point. You'll be amazed at how framing your life in this way can be empowering and enlightening. It may be a flight of fantasy, but it very subtly teaches you how to gain control of your direction.

Takeaways:

- It's easy to feel like you aren't in control of your life. After all, we literally aren't in control of anyone's actions but our own. But we must not take the easy way out by giving up control completely to externalities and other people's whims. We ultimately become powerless because we believe it.

- The first way this tends to happen is through adopting a fixed mindset. A fixed mindset is where you feel that your abilities and possibilities are fixed and limited, whereas a growth mindset accurately states that you are limited only by your efforts and actions. If you have a fixed mindset, you don't feel that things can change, so why attempt to change? A growth mindset lends itself to growth and development, knowing that effort and hard work is the catalyst.

- The second way we tend to feel powerless is through unwittingly having an external locus of control. This is when you feel that your life is fully determined by things external to you—other people, circumstances, and luck. We feel that things are predetermined and a matter of fate. This stands in contrast to an internal locus of control, where you feel that you have the power to impact your life in whatever way you wish—within reason. Again, the latter is far more associated with success because it pushes you toward achievement.

- The third and final way we might feel that we lack agency in our own lives is through adopting a helpless mindset versus a self-efficacious mindset. The former is a learned behavior that nothing will change even if you act, so therefore, you stop acting. It may have been the case once or twice, but generally, an input creates an outcome. The self-efficacious mindset is a belief in one's own abilities. This belief can be grown through personal experiences, affirmations from others, vicarious experiences, and emotional and physiological states.

Chapter 3. The Mindset of Perseverance

Surely you've heard enough comeback stories to last you a lifetime. Steve Jobs being fired from Apple, only to keep his head down, create a new technology, and come back to make Apple bigger than before. Kurt Warner working in a supermarket after a brief Canadian football career, only to come off the bench and lead the Rams to a Super Bowl championship. Tina Turner rebounding from an unthinkably abusive marriage to become a bigger star on her own terms than she ever was before.

All three of them could have given up and maybe even had greater incentive to give up than most normal people. They were publicly shamed and embarrassed, and the levels to which they'd fallen were considered impossible to bounce back from. But none of them accepted failure as a viable alternative. None of them believed that they had suffered fatal blows. They might have felt they had something to prove, but they didn't believe they were entitled to success. They blew past their limitations, tuned out cynicism, and slowly put one foot in front of the other. Well, when we do this enough, we find that we've walked miles, sometimes right to the destination we were seeking all along.

We spend a lot of time engineering our lives to avoid setbacks and failures, but this is a fool's errand. They will always come. There is never an optimal moment for them, and they will inevitably bring a host of negative emotions and disappointments with them. But the secret to creating a strong mindset isn't escaping or evading trouble: it's understanding how to power through them and set different expectations to persevere.

Doing so will help you do more than just survive in hard times—it can help you thrive.

Even in the smoothest of situations, it's still a ticking time bomb as to when you are going to hit a roadblock. We shoot for an effortless journey with no complications, but that's almost never the case, even for the simplest ambitions. "Life is tough. Get a helmet."

So what must we do to develop or find our helmet?

Turn the Obstacle Upside Down

Tragedies happen, yet the world must keep turning—and you right along with it. One of the most helpful tools to develop perseverance in the face of this reality comes from thousands of years ago.

Stoicism is an approach that transports you to directly the moment after inconvenience or tragedy strikes. How do you cope with it and survive? How can you shift your mindset to strength in the face of fire? How will you move on and extract the good from a setback instead of endlessly ruminating on your flaws?

Stoicism is a way of viewing your place in the world, and it was originally put into words by the Athenian philosopher Zeno around the third century BCE. Key to Stoicism is plain and simple perception. Consider that two people can view a horrific car accident in different ways. One person can see it as a chance for a new car while the other might only focus on the damage itself and assignment of guilt.

Perception is how we decide what events mean to us. Our perceptions can be like a lead ball chained to our feet, holding us back and making us weak, or they can be a great source of strength like a magical elixir.

How we see the world around us and how we interpret what happens to us makes a massive difference in how we get to live our lives. External events are to be treated not as good or bad but as neutral. So it's not these events, because they are ultimately neutral, but your own judgment of these events that matters.

This makes you responsible for your life. You don't control external events, but you control how you choose to look at them and then respond to them. And in the end, that's all that matters. As the famous Stoic turn of phrase says, you can *turn an obstacle upside down*. This means to look at even a negative occurrence as something that will ultimately benefit you later on or as a learning moment.

We are disturbed or delighted not by events but only by our perception of those events. What the Stoics tried to do was not get carried away by their initial impression about external events. Something happens and we automatically get an impression about it. We can't do much about that. This is our emotional reaction, but it does not have to be our overall response.

So look at what happens objectively and dispassionately—it might be raining. And then *choose* your best reaction; this is entirely up to you. The world won't end, and the activities you had planned for outdoors can be done another day. How might the rain force you to get creative or explore other untapped potential? What are the alternate perspectives you can adopt, rather than one of sadness or frustration? These alternate perspectives always exist, and you should train your ability to see them.

The truth is that you always have the ability to respond in a way that amounts to rolling with the punches. Even an opportunity to practice your sense of resiliency and patience is an alternate perspective.

Of course, it's not so simple as flipping a switch to turn the obstacle upside down and realize that your emotions are coming from entirely within you and are under your control. To be frank, most of our lives are too cushioned and comfortable for that to ever occur naturally. We have too many expectations and entitlements, and some of them are even justified. So what then?

The Stoics argued that if all we know is comfort, then we would be fragile and brittle when forced to inevitably experience pain or discomfort. By periodically practicing discomfort, we adapt and become stronger for those situations. We are able to understand that pain and discomfort are not things to be feared so much. This makes us emotionally more even-keeled.

Growth only occurs to those who are able to mentally and physically withstand discomfort. Stoicism might be the first philosophy to preach the maxim of "no pain, no gain."

Stoics were not masochist or anti-pleasure. They still enjoyed the fruits of life, but they recognized that proper perspective is needed to be nonreactive and also appreciate the good things.

Stoic philosopher Seneca puts it best:

> Set aside a certain number of days, during which you shall be content with the scantiest and cheapest fare, with coarse and rough dress, saying to yourself the while: "Is this the

> condition that I feared?" It is precisely in times of immunity from care that the soul should toughen itself beforehand for occasions of greater stress, and it is while Fortune is kind that it should fortify itself against her violence. In days of peace the soldier performs maneuvers, throws up earthworks with no enemy in sight, and wearies himself by gratuitous toil, in order that he may be equal to unavoidable toil. If you would not have a man flinch when the crisis comes, train him before it comes.

To have a chance of keeping it together in the face of adversity, you must practice. Toughen up before you need to, and you'll be prepared for anything.

Seneca suggested living as a pauper for a period of time. Wear old, unflattering clothes, eat sparsely and only plain food, and even attempt to sleep on the floor. There are various degrees to try this. You can go for a week with only simple food such as bread and soup. You can spend a month on a tight daily budget. Maybe you want to drink only water for a couple of days.

Training your discomfort muscle makes you view hardship in a different light. *Been there, done that, what's the big deal?* This allows you to detach from the circumstances and move on more quickly. You'll gain the confidence in yourself that you can handle adversity and also appreciate what you have in a powerful way. These perspectives make it difficult to overly react to negative situations.

Seneca reminds us, "It is precisely in times of immunity from care that the soul should toughen itself beforehand for occasions of greater stress... If you would not have a man flinch when the crisis comes, train him before it comes."

Instead of putting yourself in uncomfortable situations, you can also purposefully say *no* to pleasurable situations. None of this makes life harder; in fact, it makes it easier. By undertaking acts of discomfort, you harden yourself against future misfortunes. If you only know comfort, then you might be traumatized when you are forced to experience pain or any other sort of discomfort in the future, as you surely will eventually. Optimally, you'll be immune to discomfort.

Another way of training your nonreactivity and sense of gratitude is to practice negative visualization.

Stoics recommended to periodically spend time imagining that we have lost the things we value most. Imagine you have lost your family, your health, or your job—whatever you place a high value upon. Deliberately reflect on each value as if it has disappeared. Think about what you would be missing and how that would impact your daily life. Think about the despair you would feel.

Negative visualization is a powerful counter to disappointment. Suddenly, you will be forced to realize that you already have what makes you happy beyond measure. You will realize and appreciate what you have in your life, and you will also find that the desire for more has completely halted.

When you spend time deliberately realizing that everything you love and cherish could be taken from you tomorrow by some sick twist of fate, *you feel humbled.*

Finally, we must carefully distinguish between what is within our own power and what is not. Up to us are our voluntary choices, namely our actions and judgments, while *everything else* is not under our control. This means that right off the bat, you must accept that you have no control over 90% of your worries and concerns. No matter what you do or how virtuous you are, you cannot affect the outcome. So why keep your concerns dangling in your mind?

We only control our own actions and thoughts, and we have no choice but to accept the outcome. From our end, we can ensure that we are doing our best and putting our entire effort into something. But if we have done everything within our power, that's where our control really ends.

The things that are up to you, your thoughts and your actions, are the most important things in life. The most appealing aspect of Stoicism is that we are responsible for our flourishing because all that truly matters in life is up to us.

So the key lesson to take away here is to focus our attention and efforts where we actually have control and then let the universe take care of the rest. This turns out to be a very small subset of actions and thoughts, which is comforting in itself. Where a to-do list was once 10 items, you will find that it can easily be shaved down to three items.

The Stoics used the archer analogy to explain what to stop wasting your time on. An archer is trying to hit a target. He has done his best to prepare for this moment. He has practiced and trained, carefully selected his bow and arrow, and is in a state of intense mental focus. He can control each and every moment, right up until he looses the arrow. And then?

Whether or not he hits the target is not up to him. As the arrow takes flight, any number of things could happen, some predictable and some not. He may be the best archer in the world; he could simply have not prepared very well. But a gust of wind could also disrupt the arrow's path, a bird could fly into the arrow's path, or the target itself could be jolted.

None of this reflects on the archer himself. He did his best and left the rest to the flow of nature. This is all we can ever do, so we should hang our happiness and mental well-being on the shooting well instead of the outcomes we achieve.

Stoic philosopher Epictetus went on to state,

> So make a practice at once of saying to every strong impression: "An impression is all you are, not the source of the impression." Then test and assess it with your criteria, but one primarily: ask, "Is this something that is, or is not, in my control?" And

> if it's not one of the things that you control, be ready with the reaction, "Then it's none of my concern."

Check your impressions and ask yourself whether it's up to you or not. If it's up to you, then do something about it. If not, take it as it is. It was already written in stone before you got there, and it will be written in stone far after you leave. Nothing you could have done would make a difference. Picture someone who prefers chocolate ice cream but you serve them vanilla ice cream—you may have slaved over the vanilla ice cream, but that simply doesn't matter. It was never up to you, despite your efforts and planning. There is nothing left to do but move forward.

Think of your day and think of the things you have complete control of, things you have some control of, and the things you have no control of. You should eventually come to the realization that the only thing you have complete control of is yourself. The only things we control entirely are ourselves, our will, and our intentions.

You can't control if the sun will come out tomorrow; you can plan for it, but why worry about it? Focus on your own actions and improve them as you can; give yourself the best opportunity for success and the outcome you want. But in the end, a hurricane could come and destroy everything. So why worry?

Stoicism is a life philosophy that anticipates hardships. When good things happen to us, it's easy to feel strong and resilient. But it's only when we face hardship that we shape the narrative of our lives. Just like our emotions, the way we view our lives comes exclusively from us internally and doesn't really have any correlation with the reality that we live in.

A Long-Term View

To become more mentally tough, your ability to think long-term instead of focusing on the day-to-day nitty-gritty of life will prove invaluable.

Many people make the mistake of spending too much of their time focused on the immediate future or sucked into the status quo. Instead, you should consciously choose to zoom out and look at the broader picture in order to gain control over your emotions. Focusing on small setbacks that occur in the short-term can skew your view of what matters in the long-term.

Let's pretend that you had set a goal to eat more whole foods and produce on a daily basis.

On Friday, you didn't manage to eat a salad with your lunch, and on Sunday you went out with friends and ate an entire plate of deep-fried Buffalo wings. Many people may focus on the short-term and berate themselves for making such poor choices in relation to their goal. However, by choosing to zoom out and look at the broader picture, these two examples may be only tiny blips on the radar. You only have cause for concern when there are numerous blips and a pattern begins to form.

No, you didn't meet your goal on Friday and Sunday, but perhaps when looking at the entire month it will become clear that you have been making great strides toward eating more whole foods and produce on a daily basis. When looking at a single day, small deviations from your goal may loom large and seem like overwhelming setbacks. However, when you view your choices for an entire month, the true impact of an occasional small daily setback will become clear. A small setback on the daily scale does not derail a long-term goal.

By simply adjusting your perspective, you are able to identify small setbacks, such as eating a plate of wings with your friends, and move on much more quickly and with less stress and negativity. In general, if an event will seem unimportant or forgettable in a few days, then it is not worth holding on to or dwelling on.

Choosing to focus on the immediate moment causes you to engage with life in a very reactive manner: you are emotional, prone to making quick, ill-thought-through decisions, and easily derailed by day-to-day setbacks. Instead of living in this reactive manner, those with mental toughness make a conscious choice to live their lives in a state of controlled deliberateness. They are logical, measured, and consider the long-term implications of their decision before setting a course of action. Everyone encounters day-to-day ups and downs, but obsessing over short-term wins or losses is a waste of energy.

Olympic athletes are a fantastic example of individuals who shrug off short-term wins or losses to remain fixated on their long-term goals. Whether an athlete encounters a minor injury, a first-place trophy in a national competition, or unexpected training challenges, the long-term goal does not change. These small occurrences hold little weight in the face of an Olympic medal two or three years in the future. Resilient, strong individuals know that you must focus on what you can control each day, put in the hard work to move toward your goals, and live your life in a controlled, deliberate manner.

To further contrast the difference between living your life in an emotional, reactionary manner and choosing to be controlled and deliberate, consider the following scenario:

> You have $86,400 in your checking account. While getting into your car one evening, a thief approaches and robs you. He manages to steal $10 from your wallet. Would you spend your remaining $86,390 hiring private investigators and lawyers to find and prosecute the thief? Or would you recognize that in the long-term $10 means very little to you and it is better to appreciate the events that have gone well in your life and move on from this small setback?

In this scenario, choosing to find and prosecute the thief would be an example of emotional and reactionary living. It may feel good in the short-term to give in to your emotions, especially because this event might seem huge when zoomed into your timeline of the day, but it ultimately squanders your time and can negatively impact your ability to attain your long-term goals. Instead, those with mental resiliency and strength choose to think long-term.

They zoom out on their timeline and take into account what $10, a small amount of money, truly means when considering the full amount they have in their checking account. They understand that it is a waste to spend the remaining $86,390 and instead choose to move on from this short-term setback and continue making progress toward their goals.

Some of you may have made the connection that there are 86,400 seconds in one day. This scenario can also be viewed in the context of a single day. Should you waste an entire day focusing on one 10-second setback? Of course not! That would be just as wasteful as squandering $86,390. When thinking about this 10 seconds or $10 in the future, it will seem inconsequential. A small setback, when you zoom out on your timeline, becomes recognizable for what it is—insignificant.

Day-to-day wins or setbacks are inconsequential when viewed on a broader scale. Always choose to live your life with controlled deliberateness instead of allowing yourself to inhabit a short-term reactionary space.

This may not seem so powerful, but it forces you to think specifically about your future self, specifically the future self that you are aspiring to. A lot of times, we may know that we are doing something harmful in the moment, but that's not enough to stop us from doing it because we don't have any connection to our future self that will have to deal with the consequences.

Someone has just cut you off in traffic and almost caused you to crash. There was no damage done, but you are livid and on the verge of chasing them down in your car and assaulting them. What if you were to think about your mental state in 10 minutes, hours, and days? Think about what you would be doing, what you would be feeling, and where you would be if the event didn't occur.

In a sense, you are distracting yourself from the current emotional moment by reminding yourself that you have a life to live and your current rage will keep you from doing that. Control your emotions by looking ahead to the rest of your life and visualizing how you want it to go.

There is an old Zen saying: "Your anger, depression, spite, or despair, so seemingly real and important right now; where will they have gone in a month, a week, or even a moment?"

Intense emotions blind us to the future and con us that now is all that matters. In fact, when we are incredibly angry or anxious, we can even forget that there is even going to *be* a future. We've all said or done things we later regret simply because, for a time, we let ourselves be dictated by our own emotion. Look beyond the immediate and you'll see the bigger picture and calm down, too.

The 40% Rule

An easy way to think about building the skill of mental toughness is to borrow from Navy SEALs. Of course, these are elite soldiers that are known for pushing their boundaries—after all, their lives can depend on it. They intimately know that the human body and mind can push far more than we give it credit for. This is known as the 40% rule.

The 40% rule is straightforward. It says that when an individual's mind begins telling them that they are physically or emotionally maxed out, in reality they have only pushed themselves to 40% of their full capacity. In other words, they could endure 60% more if only they believed that they are capable of it. When you think you have reached your limits, you're not even close, and whether you can keep going or not depends on if you believe it. It's quite a belief to feel that you've reached your limits and say to yourself that you're only 40% done. It's an acceptance of pain and discomfort. When you stop avoiding it and embrace it, it's surprising how your perspective will shift.

We are usually ready to give up around the time that we begin to feel pain or are barely pressing our boundaries. But that point is actually just the beginning of what we are all capable of, and the key to unlocking more potential is to push through the initial pain and the self-doubt that surfaces along with it. By maintaining a belief in yourself, you show yourself that you can do more, and that evidence builds your confidence and mental toughness.

You might, for example, begin struggling after doing 10 push-ups. You'd start hearing the voice in your head that says you feel too tired, too sore, or too weak to go on. But if you take a pause and gather yourself to do one more, you find that you've already disproven the voice saying that you can't. Then you pause and do another. And then another.

And then another. Suddenly you're at 20. You can take it slowly, but you've just doubled what you thought was possible, just because you kept pushing.

Believing that you can do more will make it true, and this in itself is a skill to build. It enables you to go well beyond the limits that you've constructed for yourself in your own mind. And once you've felt the pain and the urge to give up at 10 push-ups only to push through it and do 20, you know that your mental strength helped you persevere. The next time you're challenged, you'll feel all the more capable and prepared to push past your supposed limits again. This embodies mental toughness in a nutshell—it's really a matter of how much pain you can stomach, and most of us will only bend and never break.

Our minds can be our best friends when we have a strong belief in our capabilities, but they can also be a poisonous enemy if we allow negativity to seize control. It's up to you to empower yourself using the 40% rule rather than throwing in the towel mentally at the first sign of resistance.

Imagine that you decide to run a 5k or even a full marathon despite being out of shape. Inevitably, as you run you'll begin to breathe harder, your legs will feel heavier, and you might question yourself. You could easily give up in that moment and save yourself from extra pain and soreness. But if circumstances were different and you were running away from danger out of self-preservation, you could undoubtedly continue on well beyond that first inclination to give in. Barring massive injuries, you'd finish if you believed the pain was part of the process. It's all a matter of whether you believe you can or not.

The reality is, most of us have no clue about our true physical and mental limitations. Our lives are so much safer and more comfortable than those of our ancestors, and that has some undesirable consequences when it comes to mental toughness. We don't test ourselves and we don't know what we're capable of. Now it is mostly the people who seek out intense challenges who subsequently learn discipline and mental strength while the rest go about their comfortable lives without any idea of their full capabilities.

In case you're skeptical as to the merits of the 40% rule, there is some scientific evidence in support of it that might help convince you. Numerous studies over the years have found that the placebo effect—the tangible change in performance caused merely by a belief that something you've done will impact performance—has a significant impact, especially in athletics. The legitimacy of the placebo effect suggests that your mental strength and toughness play a big role in physical abilities. In other words, if you believe it, it will *be*.

There is a scientific consensus that the placebo effect is not a deception, fluke, experimental bias, or statistical anomaly. Rather, it is a self-fulfilling prophecy in which the human brain anticipates an outcome and then produces that outcome of its own accord. In fact, the placebo effect closely follows the types of patterns you would expect to see if the brain was really producing its own desired results. Researchers have illustrated this phenomenon by showing that placebos follow the same dose-response curves as real medicines. Two pills give more relief than one, a larger pill has a stronger effect than a smaller one, and so on.

When you consider the placebo effect, it quickly becomes clear how powerful our minds are. Countless studies have supported the conclusion that the placebo effect is a result of chemical changes in the form of endorphin production. Just believing that you can give 60% more effort makes it possible.

For any goals that you have, struggles with discipline can probably be overcome by changing your expectations. Whenever you find yourself making excuses or lacking mental toughness, consider the 40% rule and the placebo effect and ask if your excuses are legitimate or if your pain and discomfort are truly significant.

Takeaways:

- Perseverance is one of the keys to what we want in life. Life is tough, so we ultimately need to develop or find helmets to get to where we want. We can't hope to get through life planning for the absence of hardship; rather, we must plan for it and plan for what to do once it happens.

- One of the best tools you can have to build mental toughness is Stoicism, a centuries-old life philosophy that is all about consciously and intentionally choosing your thoughts. The reality is that all of life's events, even the ones that we find joy in, are neutral. We are only emotionally affected because we choose to assign judgment and perspective to them. Thus, we can select to view hardship as a learning experience, and we can also train ourselves to not react through negative visualization and practicing voluntary discomfort. Finally, we must realize that there is very little in this world that we can control. Thus, all we can do is try our best and accept what comes.

- In gaining perseverance and mental toughness, we must also understand what impacts us and what does not. We are very frequently suckered into feeling urgent and immediate anxiety about negative events. But when you zoom out onto a long enough timeline, we will all die and disappear from the earth. Does this lessen the impact of daily annoyances and setbacks?

- Finally, the 40% rule as popularized by Navy SEALs is instructive to redefining our limitations. In essence, when we think we've reached our limits, we have probably reached only about 40%—not even a majority percentage. We will suffer and feel discomfort, but we will not break. We may bend, but we will still be able to get up after being knocked down. Thus, the final portion of perseverance is to expect pain and only be pleasantly surprised when it is less than you expected.

Chapter 4. The Mindset of Action

"Look before you leap" is a great maxim to follow in certain situations.

Literal leaping, for one. Knife-juggling and prescription medication as well. But when seeking to change your mindset and instill new principles to help you get to your goal, I'm strongly for the opposite—*leap before you look*. This is the mindset that places more importance on *doing* rather than analyzing or even thinking. It sounds like a risky proposition, but it's probably safe to say that you have a bit too much safety in your life.

Let's say you're working on a music platform. You have this fantastic idea for an app—it's sort of like Shazam on steroids. Not only will it identify what song you're listening to, but it will also provide you a full list of musician and production credits, along with lyrics and other information that might be relevant. You start mapping it out and telling a couple of trusted associates about it.

You're just about to start on the coding when you start questioning yourself. How are you going to obtain all this information in the first place? You're sure that if information companies saw your product in action, then they'd be happy to reach a deal to lease out that information, so why don't you just get started...

Wait a minute. Is this something modern music users really want? Who's going to stop while they're listening to a certain song because they have to know who exactly programmed the drum machine? Sure, if a potential customer saw all the information they *could* get from the app, then they'd see how much they'd enjoy using it. So get to work and…

Hold on. How are you going to convince the marketing department to make this a priority? They're too busy promoting exclusive content. They're probably going to scoff when you ask them to promote the service—it's just a list of names and instruments. Seriously? Maybe they could market it to power-users, so why don't you just go to work on the prototype and…

Uh, where's the budget coming from? Is this something you're going to work on in your free time? What if it doesn't work and…

Next thing you know, six months have passed you by, and someone else has launched an app doing exactly what yours does. It doesn't look as good as you think it should, but it was *first.* They get all the media coverage, accolades, and investment. Your project? Project over.

There's a difference between smart planning and over-caution. If we paused in our tracks to consider every potential warning or predicament, we'd spend so much time in review that we'd effectively stop what we're doing. Most people never get out of this cycle of inactivity because they find it much easier to be apprehensive than proactive. In actuality, it makes everything that much harder.

The mindset of doing and leaping before you look is an underrated aspect of getting to where you want to go. When we think excessively about the possible consequences of doing something, some may be legitimate, but 99% of them are simply excuses to prevent you from taking action. The way to break through this trap is by thinking less and doing more. Always be moving forward—the alternative is staying still or stagnating, and nobody accomplishes anything in that mode.

When you're at that juncture of moving forward or taking pause, it's always a good idea to err on the side of action and avoid the risk of stasis. Let's dive into some mindsets that will keep the wheels rolling and you on track to your goals instead of sidelined by yet another shiny object.

Thinking vs. Doing

Thinking is inactive. While it helps you realize certain facts, it doesn't make you act upon them. Thinking is the antithesis of doing, even though it may feel like you're really making headway—you're not.

Science actually suggests there's a wide chasm between thinking and doing.

Psychologists Arie Kruglanski and Tory Higgins said that humans maintain two separate but correlated orders of motivational behavior: thinking and doing. While they complement each other, the researchers suggested that we're only able to use one of those at a time.

For example, consider the activity commonly called "brainstorming," where we simply try to conjure up as many ideas as we possibly can. This mode, which they call *diverging*, employs our "thinking system." When we sift through those ideas to decide which ones are the best, the activity's called *converging* and relies on our "doing system."

Generally, we get inspired to think and act at different moments. But frequently, when we get the motivation to "do" something, we actually resort back to "thinking" mode. Thinking doesn't require much effort and is the easiest of the two activities to engage in. This is where our mindset needs to adjust more to "doing" mode. We need to get out of analysis mode and start putting energy into motion. As the study proves, this is something we need to intentionally choose to do because thinking and doing are mutually exclusive.

Making plans is fun—at least, for many of us, more fun than doing. Sorting out our plans, cataloging our wishes or daydreams, and generating ideas is sometimes the most thrilling and stimulating phase of any project. We usually emerge from such sessions energized and ready to get to work. Thinking keeps us safe from failure and lets us dwell in the fantastical and imaginary. It's a reprieve from reality.

But often that work is never followed through on if it's initiated at all. Other things come up, or other needs arise. The plans we make get relegated to the bottom of our agendas. That's the point where they get demoted. Sure, it sounded like a great idea at the time, but now that the business of daily life has taken over, that goal seems more and more impractical. We can't afford to execute on it, or we wonder if it will make any sense to do it at all.

The idea essentially withers away while it's in the purgatory of the thinking mindset. It joins a long list of other great plans and schemes that burned brightly in a minute and then died on the vine. The plans will never see the light of day. Any work that's been done on them will remain only partially complete.

That's why the "doing mindset" is so imperative. It represents the point where your thoughts translate to action. As exciting as it is to come up with new ideas, it's *much* more exciting to see them take shape in front of your eyes thanks to your concentrated work on them.

Especially in today's world in which such huge importance is given to "data-driven decisions," so many of us spend an inordinate amount of time researching, strategizing, and analyzing how to get the greatest results. In the meantime, those who are engaged in the "doing" mindset are actually producing.

Don't get me wrong—review metrics and data exactly as much as you have to. But without taking a first step, writing a first word, or hammering the first nail, all you've ended up doing is muttering to yourself pointlessly.

Granted, of all the mindsets presented in this book, the "doing" mindset is probably one of the more demanding to initiate. It involves self-discipline and dedication and certainly comes with a bit more risk. But it's far and away the best way to advance. Whatever your goal, you're not going to be able to *think* yourself into it.

Most of us will be regarded or defined by the actions we take, not the thoughts we have. And that's where you have to take the leap of courage to get out of meditative mode and snap into action mode. Don't hold yourself back because of the qualities or resources you need but don't have. If you hop into doing mode and start rolling, you'll find ways to get it done. Excuses will fade, and results will take their places.

Identify the smallest step you need to take. Think about the biggest goal you have on your agenda. Don't let how ambitious this goal seems or how much work it will take get in your way. It's not that ambitious when you think in terms of small steps. What is the first, *small* step you need to do to get this goal rolling? You'll be surprised how easy it is to keep working after you've broken ground.

For example, if you're looking to start brewing your own beer, the first step you need to take is probably studying how the whole process works. There are plenty of books you can buy that describe the process and even more websites that depict it even more succinctly. Maybe your first step is even just to clear out enough space in your garage. Those are the first and smallest steps you take before you go out and buy mash, hops, yeast, and carboys that take over your home.

Resolve to consume less, produce more. This is vital to consider right now since consumption involves more than just resources or food—it also includes massive amounts of information, distraction, and amusement. It takes more effort these days to stop constant intake. But it's far more rewarding to evolve into a mindset of production. It's not even close. It *will* help you spring into action.

Consuming, like thinking, is passive and requires no real effort. Producing something is *doing* something that's active and creative.

A good way to shift that mindset is to take a certain unit of time—one day is good, five or six days even better—and estimate how much time you spend surfing the web, watching television, playing games, or any other activity that satisfies your amusement without much in the way of giving out. Then, bit by bit, start replacing your consumption with activities with which you *produce* something. Instead of reading for two hours a night, try writing during one of those hours. Rather than watching a bunch of YouTube videos, try making a couple and posting them yourself. Again, this is a conscious shift you'll have to make at first.

Stop learning, start applying. Getting educated is one of the most important things a human ever does.

But in regards to taking action, there's only so much education you can take in before you need to start putting it to work. In fact, a handy rule of thumb is to spend no more than 50% of your time learning and at least 50% of your time applying and using.

At some point, you'll have to close the books (or websites or how-to videos) and start chiseling away at what you need to do. It might feel counterintuitive to stop learning and absorbing information, but taking the leap and applying your knowledge to action is very important. Remember, you can choose one of the two, and there are times for each. Besides, actually *doing* something is one of the most effective methods of learning anyway. It actually complements your "always be learning" mindset to start the work.

For example, if you're learning to paint, you'll probably spend a lot of your early coursework learning how to make sketches before you move on to actually using paints. There's no reason you can't make a whole series of sketches for your own purposes before moving on to the first chance you'll have to paint. For all you know, all your preplanning could go out the window or be completely wrong. Doing is actually the best way to learn because you get to combine experience with the knowledge you've synthesized beforehand.

Solution vs. Problem Mindset

This is another divide in thinking that, as you might guess, leads to either thinking or doing.

Problem-oriented thinkers consider the source or cause of the problem rather deeply, whereas solution-oriented thinkers are geared toward coming up with answers for how to fix them. Analyzing the problem is a matter of *thinking*, but searching for a solution to fix it is *doing*.

Someone with the problem-oriented mindset obsesses on the problem itself. They wonder what went wrong. They get upset that it keeps happening. They seek blame and responsibility for the problem, and the only answer they have for the problem is to "avoid it." They are unable to move past their negative feelings regarding a problem or obstacle.

People with the solution-oriented mindset seek answers about a problem, then aggressively look for ways to fix it. They don't have to remind themselves over and over that the problem is there—they know that. But staying in a feedback loop doesn't help the situation, so the solution-oriented mindset looks for answers that will work now and in the future.

There are times when the problem-oriented approach is appropriate, most commonly if one is trying to find ways to stop the problem from continually recurring. But unless we take the next step and think about how to solve the problems that come up, we're squandering that effort in the big picture.

Solution-oriented thinking takes on a different methodology toward mending a given problem. The first step is to sidestep questions that center on the problem and its causes. Asking why takes away from resolution efforts. It's just echoing the problem itself, not coming up with creative and effective solutions. Instead of asking why, the solution-oriented mindset asks, "What now?"

For example, let's say you're having a hard time grasping a certain math concept. You can spend a few minutes wondering why you're having an issue with it. If you go down that rabbit hole, you'll start wondering what the point of learning this particular concept is anyway. Why do you need to know this? What purpose will it serve in my life? With each line of inquiry like this, you're getting further away from working on the solution—which would entail going back to step one, examining how you arrived at the point you're at now, and looking for alternative routes to get to the answer.

To come up with a solution in this mindset, determine what your existing conditions are now (Point A) and how you eventually want them to turn out (Point B). By getting a clear understanding of each point and the gap between them, you'll get a much better sense of what you need to do.

Think of the problem in terms of checklists. You could make a list of everything that's going wrong. Alternatively, you could make a list that describes potential solutions. Only one of these checklists is actionable. The only actions you can derive from a list of problems are complaining and fixating on failure. With a list of actions, you have options you can immediately take. Only the action list has real value.

To practice your solution mindset, ask yourself these questions about how to handle a given job or dilemma:

- How can I solve this problem?

- How can I address this task?

- How do I get from Point A to Point B?

- What's the first step to solving this problem?

- How do I prepare to get this solution rolling?

Coincidentally, these are all questions that force you into action.

So let's say you're running a cupcake shop. Your product is tasty, but it's not selling well, at least not in comparison to other cupcake shops in the general area. The problem-oriented person would probably grouse about the situation and fixate on the trouble, so much so that they're helpless to improve it. You can check off a big list of factors that are affecting your business—location, no publicity, oversaturation of the market—but once you identify one, you have to start solving it instead of dwelling on it. You have cupcakes to make, dammit.

How can I solve this problem? By proving you have a certain edge over other cupcake makers—better recipes, more savvy publicity, developing something unique that makes you different.

How can I address this task? Let's just take the publicity angle for now. You can make catchier flyers, maybe come up with some funny (or terrible) puns for your cupcakes, look into cheap or free advertising, or have someone stand on the corner in a cupcake costume. (If Subway can do it with people in sandwich costumes, cupcake costumes can't look any more ridiculous.)

How do I get from Point A to Point B? Point A is where you are now—middling success at best. Point B is where you want to be—basically a cupcake magnate. You get from Point A to Point B by making a high-quality, well-marketed product that people go out of their way to obtain.

What's the first step to solving this problem? Sticking with the publicity angle: you look at sample advertising and marketing efforts, preferably from other, successful cupcake companies, and make note of their strategies. Then you try to adapt them to your own style so you won't be copying them and you'll look unique.

How do I prepare to get this solution rolling? Block off some time when you can research and take notes on your publicity research, think of a company, associate, or friend who would be willing to work on it (if you can't do it yourself), and find information on ad styles and rates in local alt-weeklies. Also, find where to incorporate these assets on your website. (You must have a website, right?)

I'm all in favor of quality thinking, analysis, and mental preparation for absolutely everything—but only as much as you need to start *working*. Great ideas are as much a process of experimentation, action, and solving the problems that come up in activity. With an action mindset taking precedence over a thinking mindset, you open up a virtual treasure chest of possibilities that can't come from theorizing alone.

From Motivation to Action

The final way to impart a take-action mindset is to understand the real way in which motivation appears.

It would be five-million times easier to achieve our goals if we all knew how to motivate ourselves 100% of the time. It would be like pressing a magical button that jolts us out of bed and into work. Whenever our energy is faltering, we could just press the button again, and we'd be injected with another dose of that good stuff and become correspondingly productive. The closest legal thing we have to this is coffee, but even that has waning effects.

It's easier to feel motivated when you like a project or when you're doing something you are genuinely passionate about. But let's be realistic—there are days when just the mere act of leaving your bed is a challenge and a huge accomplishment. For most of us, we don't enjoy what we do enough to feel motivated by it. An artist may be inspired and motivated to bring her visions into reality, but for the rest of us?

We're really just trying to scrape together enough willpower to get us through our days. This is all to clarify motivation's role in taking action and getting started.

Whatever your goals, motivation plays an important role and can spell the difference between success and failure. It's one of the most important ingredients to influence your drive and ambition, but we're thinking about it *all wrong*.

When we think about motivation, we want something that will light a spark in us and make us jump up from the couch and deeply into our tasks. We want *motivation that causes action*. There are a few problems with this, namely the fact that you're probably looking for something that doesn't exist, and that's going to keep you waiting on the sidelines, out of action, and out of the race. This type of motivation, if you ever find it, is highly unreliable. If you feel that you need motivation that causes action, you are doing it wrong.

For instance, a writer who feels they are unable to write without some form of motivation or inspiration is going to stare at a blank page for hours. End of story.

The truth is, you should plan for life *without* a motivating kickstart. Seeking that motivation creates a prerequisite and additional barrier to action. Get into the habit of proceeding without it. And surprisingly, this is where you'll find what you were seeking. *Action leads to motivation*, more motivation, and eventually momentum.

The more you work for something, the more meaningful it becomes to you. Your own actions will be your fuel to move forward. After you've taken your first step and have seen progress from your efforts, motivation will come easier and more naturally, as will inspiration and discipline. You'll fall into a groove, and suddenly, you'll be in your work mood/mode. The first step will always be the hardest step, but the second step won't be.

For repetition's sake, forget motivation; get started, and you'll *become* motivated. Taking the first step is tough, but consider that, aside from motivation, just getting started gives you many other things.

For instance, confidence also follows action. After all, how do you expect to be confident about something when you haven't even tried? A taste of action tells you that everything will be okay and you have nothing to fear. This is confidence rooted in firsthand experience, which is easier to find as opposed to false confidence that you get from trying to convince yourself before the fact that you can do it.

Public speaking is almost always a scary proposition. Consider how you might try to find confidence that causes action: you would tell yourself it will all be fine, imagine the audience members in their underwear, and remind yourself of your hours of rehearsal. Now consider how you might find confidence after getting started—how action can cause confidence.

"I did it and it was fine" is an easier argument to make versus "I haven't done it yet, but I think it will be fine."

The most important takeaway here is to not wait until you are 100% ready before you take the first step or that motivation is a necessary part of your process. It will probably never feel like you're completely ready. But starting down the road will motivate you more than anything else will before the fact, so allow your actions to motivate you and build confidence. Change your expectations regarding motivation, and remove the self-imposed requirements you have for yourself.

Takeaways:

- We all know we should think more. But there comes a certain point in which action is necessary. This seems counterintuitive, but studies have shown that thinking and doing are mutually exclusive. Therefore, in order to get from Point A to Point B, action is necessary, even if the steps are small and seemingly useless. You'll also have to force yourself to stop learning and consuming information to take action, but in the end, it works out better because the best way of gathering information is firsthand experience.

- You must be mindful to avoid the problem-oriented mindset; instead, strive for the solution-oriented mindset. The former simply asks why in the face of an obstacle while the latter asks, "What now?" when faced with the same. One spurs action while the other is caught in emotional meandering and fixation. Solutions are a clear point of action while problems are a refusal to move forward.

- Finally, we often confuse what it actually takes to get us feeling good about action. To be specific, most of us feel that we are seeking out motivation that creates action. But this is wrong and, in fact, in reverse. We will never be able to find a compelling reason or motivation to do things; it is unreliable at best and nonexistent at worst. So we should be using action itself to create momentum and then motivation.

Chapter 5. The Mindset of *Belief*

This chapter is about the power of belief and daring to dream, as opposed to accepting mediocrity and settling for simply what's in front of you. If you can dream something, it's more possible to achieve it than you think. But many of us suffer from limiting beliefs and obstacles that only exist in our own minds. We need to break out of those constraints and develop the mindset that helps us believe and make things possible.

Dreaming gets a bad rap. Not all dreams are simply unattainable fantasies or wishful thinking that we should snap out of. They can be powerful projections of what we most value and the ideals we're most willing to work for. Only people who are content with the ordinary try to shoot down the dreams of others.

Unfortunately, we're not encouraged to dream much in real life. Along with the skepticism of cynics, there are our own deeply held belief systems and attitudes that keep us from shooting for our best-case scenarios. We usually opt for the path of least resistance or, for some, the path with the lowest potential for pain. We start by doing this consciously out of regard for our physical or psychological safety, but if we're not careful, it becomes an instinct to hold back on just about everything.

In reaching your goals, giving your dreams a seat at the table is a huge part of changing your mindset.

It's almost impossible to do a Google search on "impossible dreams" without having J.K. Rowling come up as a result, and by now her story is probably fairly familiar. But it's a good one. Convinced at a young age that she was going to be a writer, Rowling went through a trying adolescence and a difficult early adulthood. She came up with an idea for a fantasy series while on a commuter train from Manchester to London, where she worked.

Rowling eventually found herself as a single parent without a job, forced to live on the British welfare system. "By every usual standard, I was the biggest failure I knew," she once said. She frequently wrote chapters of her book in a café with her infant daughter sleeping nearby.

She submitted her book to publishers and got the typical writer's load of rejection letters before a small publishing house in London agreed to put out her first novel, *Harry Potter and the Philosopher's Stone*. Three days after it was published in England it was licensed to an American publisher for $100,000—at the time an unheard-of sum for a children's novel.

I'm pretty sure I don't have to tell you how successful Rowling's creation became: seven novels in the series, made into eight successful movies, theme parks, merchandising, prequels, sequels, and websites where you can find out what house of Hogwarts you belong to. (I got Ravenclaw and I'm still ticked off about it.)

Rowling's initial dream might not have been as gigantic as Harry Potter-mania has become over the last two decades, but she never abandoned it, even at her darkest moments. It was a challenge to maintain that mindset, but it paid off. She may have been lucky, but leading with a dream and thinking big make people luckier on quite a consistent basis.

Think Big

Think back to when you were a child. What did you dream of becoming or doing? Even if adults tried to temper your expectations (and many did), you still had big ideas. You believed that you would eventually be able to fit in those big spaces.

As you grew older you probably adopted a more realistic approach about what you wanted to do, and your mindset followed through. Certainly, most of us have maintained that mindset because we *think* it's essential for survival: *be cognizant of your boundaries, know your limits, don't overreach or inflate your ambitions.*

And yet it can be damaging in many ways. Achieving results, thriving, and, yes, even surviving is much more dependent on being able to think big. It's how we discover exactly what we can do and how much we can achieve. Anything we could call "success" benefits from developing a mindset that welcomes the audacious, the visionary, the impossible, and—if we do it right—the crazy. Remember the self-fulfilling prophecy: you'll be as successful you think you'll be. Your beliefs and thinking will always be the cap of your accomplishments—so make that cap higher.

The first obstacle in the path to thinking big is to understand what's holding you back— your limiting beliefs. These are all your self-criticisms, doubts, or misgivings you have about your capabilities. They're the reasons or excuses you use to explain why you can't or won't do certain things. You don't have a big enough vocabulary to write a book. You don't have the money to invest in learning a craft. You're not able to multitask to plan a big project. You're too short-winded to swim.

When you settle into the think-big mindset, these limiting beliefs get smaller and smaller. As you establish your self-belief and confidence in this mindset, the limiting beliefs eventually vanish. One such method is the *BHAG*.

How big can your thinking go? And how do you get it to go that big? Authors James Collins and Jerry Porras developed a series of thought models organized around what they called the "Big Hairy Audacious Goal," or BHAG (pronounced BEE-hag) for short. The BHAG pushes companies to shape their objectives around goals that seem fantastical and ridiculous at first glance.

Most companies make goals that are pretty lackluster. They set numerical goals over a period of time, often many years in the future. They *think* doing so makes their workforce cooperate and perform more efficiently. These goals are often expressed as hard quantitative floors: "cut the operational budget by 3% within six months," "boost revenue by 15% within two years," "increase market share by 2% within five years"—strictly numerical standards that don't exactly strike an emotional chord with anyone.

The BHAG takes a more abstract and longer view, with ambitions that deliberately raise eyebrows. Collins and Porras describe it as "an audacious 10-to-30-year goal to progress toward an envisioned future." They state that companies can have more than one BHAG at once—for example, one long-term, monster BHAG and a few with shorter time frames. If you were to forecast your next year's revenue, you would multiply it by 10 for a BHAG.

The sheer size and enormity of setting a BHAG instills possibility in the mind and gives it room to run. BHAGs encourage you to come up with drastic and far-reaching ideas rather than incremental or minor improvements. They're the polar opposite of limiting beliefs. You're empowered to envision results so grand that they border on the unrealistic. That forces you to consider what's *actually* possible (because why not?). That encourages you to figure out how to achieve it in real, concrete steps. By setting higher goals, you stand to achieve much more.

Collins and Porras illustrate the concept by identifying four different kinds of BHAG:

Target-oriented BHAG. This goal combines the traditionally quantitative aspects of goal-setting with more subjective, somewhat personal aims. The trick is making the specific numeric goals (boosting revenue, increasing market share) prospects that stir the emotions of a given team—team members should see the target as a personal inspiration. It might take a certain amount of crafting to make those numbers exciting and require a solid system of evaluation to work.

This kind of group-centric goal might seem a little hard to winnow down to personal goal-setting, but it's entirely possible. You might want to set a target of getting 1,000 subscribers to your blog. You might set a goal of knitting 100 towels to sell at a market. You might want to increase the customer base of your financial consultancy firm by 10% over six months. Whatever achievement would bring you excitement and motivation works well.

Competitive BHAG. This goal rallies a team around to defeat what Collins and Porras call a "common enemy." Who's the big dog in your industry that everyone would love to see taken down? It's the classic David versus Goliath, *Karate Kid, Slumdog Millionaire*-type underdog story that's difficult to resist and easy to cheer for.

If you're a political blogger, you might harness your efforts to take down one of your ideological rivals. If you run a sandwich shop, you might want to take down the big-name franchise with stakes in your neighborhood.

Role model BHAG. This goal set is sort of a reverse of the competitive BHAG. It's where emergent organizations look to the industry leaders in their category whose success they'd like to emulate. Rather than highlight the competitive aspect, this BHAG focuses on the traits of other companies that you'd like to develop.

Going back to the examples of the competitive BHAG above, the political blogger might want to emulate the approach and promotional structure (but not the content or style) of your personal favorite writer. The sandwich shop might draw from a successful independent business that's made a name for itself in another part of town.

Internal transformation BHAG. This objective seeks a redefinition and adaptation of a company's culture and operational style. Whether it's to completely alter how a business division works or to overhaul its identity, Collins and Porras specify that it's especially useful for larger corporations trying to adapt to changing times.

All these BHAGs share one common element: they're huge. They're extremely ambitious, audacious, and seemingly impossible to achieve at the outset. But since they dispose of limiting beliefs and encourage free thinking, they open the door to endless potential. Their purpose is to transform the way you think.

Right off the bat, the BHAG model is something you may find useful to apply to your own personal life and aspirations. You're probably not overseeing the kind of large corporation the BHAG model was devised for, but you undoubtedly have as much, if not more, emotional stake in the success of your goals. And that comes from setting big-screen targets that might seem flat-out impossible or out of reach to outsiders—but aren't so far off for those who know what you're doing.

Set a revenue goal twice what you were projecting previously. Try to reach 10 times the previous year's milestones. Attempt to scale a huge mountain. Set the intention to lose 100 pounds. Strive for chopping 100 logs into firewood where you would normally chop only 20.

And then—this is the important part—contemplate exactly what you'll need to change about your current methods and processes to create those realities. When you operate with BHAGs in mind, you imagine and draw up your plans in a new way that trickles down to your everyday life. Your blueprints get bigger in relation to the size of your goals—at least it gives you a fighting chance because you have visualized and thought it over. It can be a serious game-changer.

Systems vs. Goals

Allowing yourself to dream hopefully makes you want to find ways to achieve it, and that's where the idea of system-oriented thinking comes in. It pushes you toward action because it deconstructs each goal into a system of daily tasks.

Goal-oriented thinking makes the final result the main infatuation but doesn't always consider how to achieve that goal. Merely having a goal in mind is actually what prevents us from action quite frequently because there's no action in place to reach it. A goal by itself is just a star in the sky.

The system-oriented mindset centers on specific actions that, if done on a consistent basis, will naturally get you close to any goal you set. It emphasizes consistent action—small daily tasks and duties that make motion easier to fathom than striving toward huge, insurmountable goals.

A system is a set of procedures, routines, and processes that you follow to achieve the desired goal. Ideally, this system is proven and repeated and produces the same, or very similar, outcome every time it runs. There are systems for virtually every aspect of our existence—exercise circuits, method acting, math functions, medical procedures, hairstyling. Name it, and there's a process to it.

On the other hand, a goal is the summation of your efforts, the pinnacle of your achievement—which means it comes loaded with stress and anticipation.

For instance, you may have the goal of becoming a painter. But a goal alone doesn't address *how* you make that goal real. The system mindset considers what's needed to become a painter—the education, the practice, the supplies you'll need, the steps you'll need to achieve your goal. Complete X, Y, and Z over a certain amount of time and you'll automatically fulfill your goal.

Highlighting the system mindset over the goal mindset can be more drastically advantageous than you might think and can make your dream become more realistic bit by bit. In the spirit of this chapter, you can also think bigger with your daily systematic actions. If you're a pro golfer, then your goal is to win a tournament. But what kind of system do you have to employ for yourself to make that goal a reality? What consistent actions build the ladder to winning more tournaments? How can you build upon them?

Your system is going to consist of some combination of early-morning training, practice with coaches, and refinement. Focus your efforts on simply completing the duties you need to complete, and you'll be better off. Think of it as a formula that moves you ahead in life and toward whatever you want to achieve.

Systems thinking lessens the pressure by helping you keep centered on the simpler, everyday processes that help you build on your skills over time rather than on the burden of the gigantic, big finish you want. Systems force you to take it step by step on a daily, gradual basis. The beauty of this is that you'll make improvements and develop better habits—whether or not you ultimately obtain your goal.

A system is not a 100% foolproof roadmap for success. Inevitably there will be days when you work on the system a little harder than others. If you're on an exercise program, you'll run longer on certain days than you will on others. But in a good system, you will do *something* every day. You will develop the discipline that will eventually bring you much closer to your goal. There will be days when you step on the scale and won't notice any difference—but a good system accounts for that. As long as the system produces a net success rate, it's working.

Focusing on a goal, however, imposes some unexpected restrictions. True, it's much more likely that you'll attain a single goal if you concentrate on it exclusively. But you also might miss an experience that might have been even better than your target. A system that works toward your goal but is ultimately independent of it increases your chances overall. Your vision in a system isn't so trained on one specific object that you'll miss out on another prospect. Anything is game in a system mindset.

There are some exceptions in which goals are helpful. If you're intent on being a physician and you have the innate talent for it, then keeping close to your goal is vital. But most of us don't have such a clear long-view plan. We don't know what's going to happen, what chances will come our way, or what we'll have to do to get to them. The best that *we* can do is get into a situation where the odds are more favorable—a place with more possibilities, more chances to improve a skillset, more opportunities for networking, and the chance to experiment in different subjects.

To build a systems mindset, think in smaller, gradual steps instead of massive or drastic measures. Give yourself credit for each step you take toward achieving your goal, not the grand prize for the goal itself. Appreciate the gradual experience for what it can bring to other areas of your life and the opportunities it will open. This mindset will patiently and meaningfully bring your dreams closer to reality.

The Alter Ego

If you're struggling with belief in yourself, and refusing to see your limitless possibilities, then it might be time to don an alter ego to help.

Have you ever put on a mask for Halloween? Everyone you came into contact with that day knew you were wearing a mask. They might have even known it was you behind it. But admit it: wasn't it just the least bit *empowering*?

One of the best ways to create a sense of belief is by creating an alter ego because of the surprising feeling of power and control it can give you. During Halloween, you might feel emboldened and empowered by wearing a mask or costume—imagine how great it would be to apply that sort of feeling to everyday situations.

Anonymity gives us a sense of bravery, and this is best showcased in today's social media and online world. When we lurk behind a fictitious screen name, we unchain ourselves from the restrictions of our own, real-world identities. We speak through another voice, almost like a ventriloquist speaks through the dummy on his lap. We may express things we'd never say in the real world. This is what scientists call the "online disinhibition effect."

A recent survey conducted by the audience engagement platform Livefyre reinforces that conclusion. The company, which powers user-content features for major web entities, asked 1,300 web users if they've ever commented anonymously online and why.

Most said they did so because they didn't want their opinions to impact their work or professional life by being attached to their real names. They also responded that they wanted what they *said*, the actual content of their message, to be the focus of the post rather than their identity. Almost 80% said if a site forced them to log in with their true identities, they wouldn't comment at all. Seems that perceived anonymity isn't just empowering; it's necessary for most people.

This is the same effect you can create (in a nicer way) when you create an alter ego. Alter egos can be a hidden side of your personality, an exaggeration of what you really believe, or someone totally opposite from who you are. The underlying point is that you feel exponentially more freedom and belief, sensing yourself to be immune from retribution or harm in the real world.

Used properly, an alter ego can help nudge you closer and closer to the edges of your comfort zone and allow you to express your beliefs and big goals for the first time in your life.

An alter ego is a second self created by an individual, usually for the purpose of living out a "better" version of the self.

In comic books, Bruce Wayne runs his multimillion-dollar business every day. Peter Parker works as a photographer for the *Daily Bugle*. But when a crisis hits the cities they live in and the usual authority figures are unable to handle it, they morph into their crime-fighting alter egos Batman and Spiderman. The city is saved, usually with a little property damage, but still saved.

Pop music artists, in particular, are frequent adopters of the alter ego. When they take the stage, they have to push out a larger-than-life spectacle that takes more than their everyday, regular selves to pull off. All pop musicians do that to some extent, but some go even further by creating elaborate personas.

For a time, the great British performer David Bowie changed personas seemingly at will. The best-known was Ziggy Stardust, a humanoid alien who's something of an extraterrestrial messenger. Ziggy let Bowie distance himself from the boy from Beckenham and take on a fearless, heroic personality.

An alter ego encompasses the best parts of what you want to be and gives you full license to do what you couldn't do as yourself. At the very least, it allows you to ask what someone else would do and witness the separation between your answer to the same question.

An alter ego that's thought out well can help you bridge the gap between where you are now and where you want to be. It lets you step out of the box you've created for yourself and do something that's totally out of character. The imaginative process you take in creating and being that alter ego might provide clues on how to make those improvements in your real life. Finally, it just lets you ask, "What would my fearless alter ego do?" This is a more productive question to answer than, "What should I do here if I know I should be brave but am still scared?"

Having an alter ego, as we've mentioned, is empowering. After switching characters, you have a window of opportunity when you can be brave and detach yourself from your hang-ups. That window of time is when you push against your comfort zone and try new things.

An alter ego can give you some distance from yourself and help you deal better with the past, present, and future. When you think of your alter ego, you're more likely to make good decisions on their behalf. The self-distance and objectivity you create when taking on this alter ego, and thinking about what he or she would do, can sharpen your focus on the bigger picture and make some of your long-term goals a little clearer.

When it comes to the future, you might be more willing and eager to take on challenges if you picture your alter ego doing them instead of yourself. For the moment, your alt-self will be the one taking the chances, facing obstacles, and risking failure. It won't be you, for now. But when it finally becomes your turn, you'll be more prepared to handle it, thanks to what your alter ego set up for you.

Every time you're about to try a new endeavor to create a new belief about yourself, there's a little voice in your head that begins whining and advising you. This is your actual ego, the one Freud described. Its job, as we discussed earlier, is to be the reasonable one in any new situation.

And when faced with a new situation, your ego gets a little jittery: "What are you doing? Stop! What if you look stupid? What will everyone think? What if they all laugh at you? Who do you think you are, anyway—you're not brave or smart or strong enough to do this! Let's just go home and watch *The Little Mermaid* again!"

That's when an alter ego comes to the rescue, bolts past your ego's whimpering, and leads you out of the comfort zone. Where the ego expresses fear, the alter ego is rarin' to go. "Hey! This looks great! This looks exciting! Let's get started now!"

The ego then says, "But what will everybody say? You're just setting this person up for ridicule!" To which the alter ego responds, "Oh, forget them. If they don't have anything better to do than gossip, let 'em talk. They can think whatever they want. It's not going to get in our way. I got no use for 'em."

Finally, the ego cries, "But what if I *fail*?" And the alter ego says, "If you try it, yeah, you might fail—but you might *succeed*—whereas if you *don't* try, then you'll *definitely* fail. Excuse me, I'm running late."

Your results—and inner dialogue—may vary. Not only are you speaking in the terms of your alter ego, but you're also treating your *comfort zone's* ego as an objective, other character as well. You can verbalize what you want to change about your comfort zone and let your alter ego run with it.

Determine why you want an alter ego. Ask yourself what's spurring you to develop an alter ego and what you hope to achieve. Do you want to be more outgoing, confident, or unique? Do you need someone to stand up for you? Do you just want more people to read your blog or watch your YouTube videos? In what way will they be assisting in breaking you out of your comfort zone?

Your alter ego should have some sort of purpose or mission. Remember, you're looking for empowerment, an avenue by which you can express yourself in a new context. You're putting your hopes, dreams, fears, and insecurities into this alter ego, giving them the kind of abilities that you don't have as a mortal human. Your alter ego doesn't necessarily have to live by the rules, but it should have a *point.*

Develop your alter ego's personality. What type of person does your alter ego have to be to achieve the goals you're after? How do they think? What's their mindset? What models are you using to build their thoughts or actions?

You have an unlimited range of options to choose from. You could just use the alter ego as a reflection or extrapolation of yourself to imbue a personality that you'd like to someday inhabit. Conversely, you can make it your polar opposite to investigate a total contrast of yourself to help you understand the "other side." The answers you're looking for are largely going to come from the type of attitudes and voice your alter ego has, so develop them as fully as you can.

Make sure you can describe your alter ego, without hesitation, using five positive adjectives. These are the traits you are striving toward.

Flesh out the details. The secondary part of your alter ego's story will be how they'd present themselves to the rest of the world—so give them a name and an appearance. Again, you have no restrictions here. You might be a T-shirt and jeans person, but your alter ego could be a high-fashion hound all the way with garish fur coats and sparkling sunglasses. Or perhaps they'll only wear black and disappear underneath the hood of their sweatshirt.

Spend time developing your alter ego's mannerisms. How do they walk? What does their voice sound like? How do they wear their hair, or do they wear hats? Do they speak the King's English, or do they have some kind of accent? The more details you can provide for your alter ego, the easier it will be to slip into their character.

Try to come up with a significant and meaningful name. You can base it on someone you admire, the name of your superhero, a take on another fictional character, or one from history. You could just attach a superlative to the end of your name—"Felix the Great"—or spell your name backward. Have some sort of justification or explanation for the name, even if it's random. As with appearances, the more detail you can invent, the more tangible the alter ego will feel.

Activate! An alter ego should respond to some kind of call to action, something to invoke them when they're needed. Captain Marvel called out to his gods, who then graciously struck him with lightning and turned him into a superhero. Batman was channeled into action by an extremely powerful, custom-made flashlight that seemingly every household in Gotham had. The alter ego rock band KISS took to the stage with the announcer's cry "You wanted the best... you *got* the best! The hottest band in the world, KISS!"

You could come up with a rallying cry, something that could theoretically fit on a T-shirt or hat. You could cue up a song that would announce the alter ego's arrival or something that would just pump you up. You could throw red roses in its pathway, unfurl a flag or carpet, clang on a cowbell—whatever works.

The activation routine is important because it's meant to snap you out of your mood and take on the alter ego's spirit. If you feel sad, it's extraordinarily difficult to just "decide" you feel happy. Some sort of catalyst, calling, or benediction can help turn that alternate mood on.

Remember, this isn't just escapism. A lot of people do role-playing or cosplay for recreational reasons. While you should have fun with your alter ego, you're not just creating it to escape into a fantasy world. You invented it to figure out a solution of some sort to achieve a certain goal.

You know how *you'll* act. That's why creating a distance from that is important. Your alter ego encourages you to act more quickly, more sharply, and more bravely because you're taking yourself out of the picture. You're not thinking about yourself anymore. You're thinking about a woodland nymph, an astronaut, Marilyn Monroe, and the Incredible Hulk now.

Takeaways:

- The mindset of thinking big is where you attempt to completely bypass your limiting beliefs. When you dare to think big and dream, you may find that you achieve much more simply by planning for it. One way to do this is by thinking in terms of BHAGs—big, hairy, audacious goals. Instead of shooting for X, shoot for 10X and rethink exactly what's possible and necessary.

- Thinking big, however, does not stand alone, and that's where systems thinking comes in. Think in terms of a system instead of a goal; a system is merely a series of consistent tasks, whereas a goal is a one-time occurrence or achievement. Focus on the small actions that the system dictates and you will find yourself closer to your goals as a matter of circumstance.

- Finally, an alter ego has the surprising power of completely changing your perceptions and beliefs. That's because it's not you. Your alter ego, to be most effective, should represent your ideal self. What do you wish you were more or less of? What traits are you seeking? What beliefs do you want to embody? That's what your alter ego should epitomize because you already know what *you'll* do in certain situations and it's something you want to change. Conveniently, the alter ego also serves as a buffer to our sense of ego and pride.

Chapter 6. The Mindset of Gratitude

Having gratitude is one of the most valuable mindsets we can have. Chances are, there are at least a few things in your life that you're thankful for, things that are keeping your head above water or are giving you some measure of happiness.

And yet, sometimes, we can be so ungrateful and miserable in a way that can ruin our day. Why? Maintaining that sense of gratitude and verbalizing it whenever you can keep you centered in your reality and happier overall.

I knew someone a while ago who went through an unexpected, prolonged period of extreme depression. Several things in their life seemed to be imploding at the same time: the end of a long-term relationship (and their ex almost immediately starting a new one), the loss of a job, having to move to a completely new apartment with almost no furnishings, and a general withdrawal from almost all social contact.

This person went total recluse one time after the holidays. They didn't go out to the places we used to meet up, and they made no attempt at communication—they just went off the grid completely for about three months. No one knew how they were doing. Some of us thought we'd never see them again.

Then they just showed up again at the café we hung out at. No warning, no notice, just back in the fray. And they seemed a lot more at peace than we'd ever seen them before. Within a month from that time frame, it was as if they'd become a completely different person.

A few years after, I reminded them about that time and asked how they'd gone from such a painfully dark place to a substantially better one in a relatively brief time.

"Two things," they said. "First, I took a hard look at why I'd had so many failures happening and why I'd taken them so personally. I realized the problem was that I went into everything with a certain *expectation*. And I mean everything: jobs, relationships, friendships, socializing—I did everything with some kind of *motive*. Whether I said it or not, I demanded something back. I realized that was a pretty ineffective and selfish way to conduct one's life.

"The next thing was that I decided to just stop doing that and that I'd consciously try—just for a little bit of time—to be more generous with my friendships, more positive about them, and try to get outside my selfish bubble and actually try to *help* people, with no expectations that I'd get anything in return. I needed to be positive and steer things toward an optimistic outcome. That's all. That was my game plan.

"I figured I'd try it for a couple of weeks, maybe a month. But it worked so well that I couldn't stop. Didn't want to."

Gratitude is not easy when we're in a bad place. When we don't have what we think we want, the last thing we want to do or hear is "be thankful for what you already have." At best, it's useless advice; at worst, we might even take it as an insult.

That said—be thankful for what you've got, because it is impossible to feel simultaneously negative and grateful. Wouldn't it be nice to approach the world from a positive and happy perspective by default? We often forget that we control our own feelings and that being angry or being grateful is nothing more than a selection—you can *choose* which one you want to be.

Create Perspective

The right perspective on gratitude benefits the mindset because it instills positivity as a regular approach. That gives you the energy to change and affect situations in a way negativity cannot. The advantages of being grateful are real and unambiguous—they're even backed up by science.

Gratitude makes us happier. Gratitude, simply put, begets more gratitude, which in turn generates more joy. A study conducted by the University of Miami and UC Davis showed that keeping a five-minute "gratitude journal" can boost your happiness by 10%. The general idea is that expressions of gratitude trigger "feedback loops" of more gratitude. Just by unexpectedly thanking someone or merely making a mental note of gratitude, the benefits could start immediately. You just have to make the first move and your brain will do the rest.

For example, if you expressed gratitude to a friend simply for being a positive influence in your life, it would generate more gratitude—especially if your friend responds positively and might be influenced to "pay it forward," creating more pods of happiness in their own life. You might even just decide to compare what you currently have to your equivalent from a war-torn country, and you'll suddenly gain perspective on your life.

Gratitude makes people like us. In 2006, researchers Emily L. Polak and Michael E. McCullough found that people who were 10% "more grateful" than average had 17.5% more "social capital." This increased sociability bettered their opinions about their immediate surroundings and also helped other people accumulate more social capital as well.

I've experienced this firsthand—when I've expressed gratitude for a mere friendship or someone's returned the compliment, it almost always results in a tighter and more meaningful circle of friends. When you extend small, unexpected favors—like a thank-you note, a personal gift, or some other means of expressing gratitude for someone being in your life—people naturally consider you a friendly person.

Gratitude makes us happier. A 2005 study from *American Psychologist* found that just one single act of *gratitude*—even just feeling or expressing it—resulted in a 10%

increase in happiness and a 35% reduction in symptoms of depression. Further, people who wrote down three good things that had happened to them in their day every night for a week showed more sustainable positive impact—even weeks after they'd stopped journaling.

Gratitude makes us more optimistic. In the same Miami–UC Davis study mentioned above, participants who kept a weekly gratitude journal also exhibited a 5% increase in optimism. People who kept a *daily* gratitude journal showed a 15% increase. Optimistic people were almost biologically programmed to focus on the positive aspects of life, whether it's being thankful, laughing, showing kindness, or forgiving. Gratitude is an almost self-generating form of hopefulness.

Gratitude makes you friendlier. A study from Southern Methodist University, UC Davis, and the National Institute for Healthcare Research determined that gratitude promoted pro-social behavior. Participants who kept a gratitude journal were more likely to help other people with their issues and were more relied upon for positive emotional support. Just as gratitude can increase your social reach, as seen above, it also makes your communal circle *stronger*.

This gratitude sounds like a pretty fantastic product. How can we consciously promote a feeling of gratitude more often in our lives? The website Unstuck.com offered a few suggestions in this direction.

Notice your daily world from the standpoint of gratitude and allow yourself to be astonished by all the kindness and abundance we take for granted—whether it's appreciating a nice-weather day, the friendships you have, or the fact that you can buy a candy bar at a convenience store. And of course, if all else fails, compare your status quo with that of someone in far less fortunate circumstances than yours.

Maintain a gratitude journal, as some of the above studies suggest. All you need to do is make a note of a couple of things you're thankful for on a daily basis, whether it's online, on a notebook, or on paper. You can write in it daily or weekly, and it doesn't have to be a long narrative—just five or so simple, short phrases about what you appreciate.

Compliment someone at least once every day. This can be direct praise to someone or just your general appreciation of something positive ("I love how quiet it is in the morning," "I love the smell of the air after it rains," etc.). Positive reinforcement and affirmation always make one feel better, whether they're generating or receiving it. You'll feel great from doing it and be motivated to continue.

When you're in a bad situation, ask yourself what you can learn from it. Accept and own your feelings about it, but try to pivot from self-blame or despair by realizing you've absorbed a life lesson. It's not only a failure or setback; it's an opportunity for learning. In the future, when you look back on this moment without too much emotion, ask what you'll be grateful for. If you've recently ended a bad relationship, lost a job, or received some form of rejection, try to separate yourself at some point and answer what it's taught you about how life works.

Make a commitment not to complain, criticize, or gossip for just one week. If you stumble a bit, just marshal your forces and keep going forward. Don't feel like one misstep will throw you off completely. Observe how much energy you were wasting on negativity and discouraging thoughts. Chances are, a good portion of your daily conversations are devoted to complaining, ranting, or raving. Our brains actually adapt to repeated negative talk and make it harder to see what you should be grateful for. You can measure your current mindset by how hard it is to keep yourself from engaging in destructive speech.

Positivity and Optimism

Feeling positive and optimistic is also a mindset choice that can benefit your fulfillment and happiness. Especially in times of global stress and worry, it's becoming a more important choice to make. Observing the world with a positive attitude and the resilience to make the best of what life has to offer have prolonged effects on our immediate outlook but also have tangible benefits over the long-term.

A couple of studies have shown how even just cosmetic alterations that reflect a positive attitude can effect meaningful change.

Smiling improves mood. Just the mere physical act of smiling—regardless of context, whether in a great mood or not—can trick your brain into feeling better. I'm not kidding—smile first, ask questions later.

In 1988, scientists from Universität Mannheim in Germany did a study about emotion but did not tell their test participants that was the focus of their study. They just asked them to hold pencils with their faces.

Participants in one group were instructed to hold the pencils vertically between their teeth. This maneuver, however awkwardly, forced them to smile. Participants in another group were instructed to hold their pencils lengthwise between their lips, which turned their expressions into frowns. Those in a final control group were just told to uneventfully hold the pencils with their hands.

If it sounds like these folks weren't having a good enough time already, the test administrators then showed them a series of humorous images. The participants who were forced to smile expressed that they found the images much funnier than those who were forced into frowning, with the control group landing in the middle.

The scientists concluded that it was easier for the subjects to exhibit joy—via laughter—if their physical muscles were "used to" do so by holding a smile. You might say that smiling is the physical manifestation of optimism, in which case it can literally improve your mood and make you happier.

Positivity and meditation prolong life. In 1989, Stanford professor Dr. David Spiegel ran a study on 86 women enduring the final stages of breast cancer. Half of the women were administered only their usual prescribed medical treatment, whereas the other half were assigned weekly support groups in addition to their regular medication. The support meetings were chances for the women to share their emotions and associate with other patients in a sympathetic environment.

After the conclusion of the study, it was revealed that the women in the support group lived twice as long as the women who only received traditional treatment. The findings were echoed in a 1999 study that showed cancer patients who generally felt powerless or hopeless had a lower chance of survival than those who felt more optimistic.

Another remarkable story involves screenwriter David Seidler, who won an Oscar for the screenplay of *The King's Speech*. Seidler had been diagnosed with bladder cancer in 2005, which had been controlled with visualization and meditation techniques. Two weeks before his bladder was to be operated on, Seidler refocused his attention and visualized being cancer-free.

When Seidler underwent a biopsy immediately before his operation, his doctor said, "I don't know how to explain it, but there's no cancer there." After comparing Seidler's pre-diagnosis biopsy with his new results and sharing them with other professionals, the doctor's proclamation that Seidler was cancer-free was confirmed. Seidler theorized that his visualizations had caused his cancer to go into "spontaneous remission." At least, that's a story worthy of a screenwriter. The scientific community has various opinions about how effective positive thinking is in improving health issues—this shouldn't be taken as a suggestion for a cure.

You know that optimism can help, and it is best summed up as building a habit of looking at things from alternative perspectives—the brighter side of things or the silver lining in the dark cloud.

Conflicts, problems, and trouble force us to choose how we approach them. We consider how we're going to concentrate and channel our efforts. There's often the impulse to seek to blame other people, society in general, or our environments. Optimists don't do that. Instead, they use the solution mindset and try to find remedies.

Think back on some of your worst breakdowns or defeats from the past. Did you take anything meaningful from them? How did what you went through change your approach so you didn't repeat those mistakes? By fairly and objectively looking back on your past failings, you'll be better able to diagnose new difficulties and be able to proactively find answers for them. If you were in a broken relationship, you might try to understand what traits you exhibited—as well as those of your partner—that you might want to consciously modify or avoid.

Many of us can't let go of our failures. We're constantly haunted by them, allowing them to compromise our self-confidence and raise a closet full of doubts. This harkens back to the problem-seeking mindset we discussed earlier. When that happens to you, simply ask yourself, "What's the one thing I could do that will improve this circumstance?" When you reinstate the solution-focused mindset, you'll get a near-immediate feeling of progress, potential, and confidence. All those serve as the basis for an optimist.

For example, if you're in an adverse situation at work—like a doomed project or a serious mistake—you'd want to describe what the ideal result would have been like, determine what steps kept it from getting that way, diagnose why they didn't happen when they were supposed to, and note how and when to improve the situation. This keeps you focused on the model you want to emulate and makes fixing it feel like a positive step.

Optimistic folks don't have any time to spend on those who would bring them down—the pessimists who deplete others of their spirit and strength. Cutting negative people out of your life—even if they're close to you—is often necessary to save your sense of positivity. In fact, you may have read these last few paragraphs and realized that you, too, might be one of those pessimistic people. We can help you with that.

Instead of living in the echo chamber of naysayers, try to cultivate relationships with people who are more positive-minded. Exchange new ideas with each other and see if you can find a way forward together. Bit by bit, you'll probably find that sourness fading away.

You'll come across other optimists since they're naturally attracted to that kind of positivity. You'll probably get so much assistance and inspiration that you'll have no idea what to do with all of it. They'll get back from you in turn, and it'll be a virtuous circle instead of a vicious one. Before any of that happens, though, you'll have to reduce or eliminate the time you spend with the negative crowd—the ones who irritate or frustrate you.

As they say at the beginning of every baseball season, "This is a marathon—not a sprint." Life is a series of miniature victories that compile over a period of time. When considering the meaning of your life, it's good to take the long view: weeks, months, even years. Your emotions will likely level out and be more positive when you ponder the longer frames of time. Limiting your view to what's happening right now tends to redouble the negative emotions you might be feeling.

For example, if you're starting a new business, you may be mired in certain steps you have to take to get rolling. You have to apply and wait for business licenses, figure out how you're going to generate income, determine how you're going to market yourself, and endure not getting a huge number of customers for a while.

The "sprint" mindset would make you exhausted with all this activity and might make you question whether it's really worth it. But the "marathon" mindset understands these are all necessary steps that almost every single business in the free market has had to go through. After you become successful, you'll understand why it was worth it.

Pay attention to how you've changed. Ask yourself what you've learned and in which areas you've gotten better. Write them down, record them, or just meditate on them when you're going about your day. Like any skill or mindset, self-confidence is something you have to exercise, as much as you must work for physical fitness or developing a habit. When it gets to be a routine, you'll be able to maintain it more easily over time. Noting your progress will feel like a normal thing you do every day.

Another effective way to support this practice is to catalog your successes at the end of each day. Simply reflect and ask yourself, "What did I do well today?" All this does is fortify your optimism as a matter of daily practice. As your daily answers amass day by day and week by week, your self-confidence will only amplify and lay the groundwork for your success.

Similarly, inject optimism at a higher level by commemorating improvement when it happens, even if the progress is small or others might consider it insignificant. If you're trying to lose 50 pounds, take a victory lap if you've only managed to lose half a pound. Be grateful to yourself for making progress whenever you can.

It's easy to laugh off the idea of positive thinking and optimism as Pollyanna-ish, giddy cheerleading. (At least you're laughing!) But there's ample support for the notion that such adjustments can literally change one's mentality, initiative, and even physical health. Not only that, but it's astonishingly cost-effective. Smiles don't cost anything, but they're never cheap.

Takeaways:

- It is virtually impossible to be grateful and unhappy at the same time. Seek to inject this type of happiness into your daily life. Bad things happen every day, and yet some people are more resilient. This is because of gratitude and the power it has to eliminate negative thoughts.

- Gratitude has been shown to create a host of physical and psychological benefits. Those aren't important; rather, it's more important to understand how to show daily gratitude. You can do this by complimenting others, seeking perspective, asking what you can learn from setbacks or failures, and making a commitment to not complain or give voice to your negative thoughts.

- Optimism, even if you have to force it at first, has also shown a host of benefits. Smiling can literally change your body's chemistry, and everything else about optimism can best be summed up as cultivating the habit of looking at the bright side of things. To stay positive, optimistic, and grateful, cut out negative people from your life, understand that life is a marathon, pay attention to your changes and improvements, and try to embrace a solution-oriented approach.

Chapter 7. The Mindset of Humility

There's nothing like a true sense of pride in accomplishment, reaching a goal you've worked to achieve, and feeling the elation of success. Everyone craves that emotion. After we get to that point of satisfaction and live in it for a little while, it's always a fantastic idea to restate a very specific affirmation: *I know nothing.*

"Wait," you're saying, "I just gave you six chapters of my life, and once I reach my destination, you're telling me I don't know anything? Are you trying to get me to buy the sequel to this book?"

No, I'm not, though please feel free to buy as many of my books as you like. I'm saying that while your accomplishment has been made, your journey isn't done. Actually, it's just started, and you have many levels of depth and insight to peel back—in theory. Whether it is literally true or not, imagine yourself as always being on a path until you are literally drawing your final breath. By ascending to the top of where you want to be, you're actually just opening up to more opportunities to learn, be humble, listen, and understand how very little you truly know.

The ultimate and most valuable mindset to have is one of perpetual and humble *learning*. Similar to the growth mindset, willing to be humble and putting yourself in a lower tier of knowledge relative to others helps you appreciate experience, increase your personal insight, and strengthen your confidence. It also helps to remove the fear, inadequacy, or other stress that sometimes comes with our encounters with the unfamiliar.

Adopting a learning mindset shouldn't be a blow to the ego, although it sounds like you should devalue yourself in favor of others.

What you're doing is not related to your ego—it's just putting yourself in a position to be able to listen to others and keep improving yourself bit by bit. The ego hates to admit it, but imagine how much differently you would act if you could just state with a straight face, "I'm willing to hear you out and really listen to you." Your chances of continued success run much higher with that mindset than with one that's closed off to learning.

Letting go of your ego in a relationship, for example—realizing you can't know everything about the person you're with—helps foster understanding and a free exchange of emotions and information, and it certainly deescalates potential flare-ups. Putting aside ego and humbling yourself to admit that you indeed were the one to make an error makes a bad situation better because people will see how honest of a coworker you are.

This chapter is about putting your ego on pause and how to accept that none of us are ever a finished product. How do you become a more finished product?

The Beginner's Mindset

The mindset of a beginner—even to the point of considering yourself a novice or amateur in something you've known about for years—is extremely beneficial in helping you view the world as a learning grounds to finish the product of *you*.

A common misconception about being an "expert"—even among experts—is that it implies you don't have to learn anything anymore. You've reached the fullest extent of knowledge possible in a given situation, and any suggestion that you could still learn more is almost insulting. You think—or feel—that you've already transcended all limitations and that there's nowhere to go but down.

However, ideally, there's not much difference between a beginner's mindset and an expert's mindset. That's because when someone decides they want to become an expert on any subject, the first thing they have to accept is that they will *never stop learning* about that subject. Long after they've established themselves as an authority about that subject, they will still be learning about it and discovering just how much they still don't know. An expert never stops wanting to fill in those gaps. The expert and the beginner therefore share an openness to new knowledge and insight.

The beginner's mindset is drawn from the Zen Buddhist concept *Shoshin*, which is described as "having an attitude of openness, eagerness, and lack of preconceptions when studying a subject, even when studying at an advanced level, just as a beginner in that subject would."

Every time you come across a new situation, no matter how shopworn or streetwise you think you are, reorient yourself to experiencing it as a beginner. Release all of your preconceived notions or expectations about the experience. Treat it with curiosity and a sense of wonder as if you were seeing it for the first time.

As a quick illustration, imagine you see a herd of zebras outside of your bedroom window—hopefully a novel situation for you. Once you get over your initial shock, what are your initial observations and questions?

Does this situation remind you of something you're already familiar with or have seen in a movie, perhaps? You'd try to make sense of it all and construct and narrative to understand it through. What happened beforehand and what will happen after? What details are surprising or downright odd when you think about it beyond first glance? You'd certainly focus on "why" and "how" questions. You would probably also be overwhelmed with sensation and stimuli.

Now let's take another example of learning how to play a new instrument. What questions would you ask? Where would you even start? You wouldn't know what's important, so everything would seem significant at first. You'd probably be curious as to the limits of the instrument—first in how to not break it and then in its overall capabilities. You'd be filled with wonder and also caution for fear of making an error or breaking it. The impression it makes on you immediately won't be forgotten for a very long time.

Those are the underpinnings of the beginner mindset. When you try to reprogram your mind to a blank slate and act as if you truly have no knowledge about something, knowledge will come far easier than acting like you do through the form of extensive questioning and curiosity.

It should be emphasized that the beginner's mindset empowers the ability to ask *dumb questions*. So-called experts rely on assumptions and their own experiences, often without further investigation. When you feel comfortable asking *dumb questions*, nothing is left up to assumptions and chance, and everything is out in the open and clarified.

You can approach both new *and* familiar situations with this same principle. Next time you're driving a car, try noticing the things you would automatically do otherwise and say them out loud to yourself. Along with that, focus on what you sense when you're behind the wheel but have long since stopped paying attention to: the ridges in the steering wheel, the glow of the dashboard odometer, or the sound of the air conditioner. Even these crushingly insignificant details could unlock and reveal some new element or impression that you've never experienced before.

The beginner's mindset requires slowing down and paying attention to what you've ignored for a long time.

"I Know It All" vs. "What Don't I Know?"

Like the beginner's mindset, the intellectually curious mindset ("What don't I know?") is almost synonymous with the expert mindset (in my expert opinion, anyway). The difference is that the intellectually curious mindset is aggressive about finding answers, learning more, and absorbing as much knowledge as we can about different issues, principles, and beliefs—especially ones that run counter to our own. This kind of assertive approach to discovering new information is an effective means of staying humble and allowing yourself to improve while your ego is on sabbatical.

The key is to regard everyone you know and meet as a potential spring of knowledge, someone who can tell you something you didn't know every time you encounter them. Actually, more than a spring of knowledge—a *huge* spring of *fascinating* knowledge.

The intellectually curious person does not stop pursuing the answer to the question "Why?" They don't settle for the standard party-line answers they get at surface level—they get more integral and exact until they've uncovered the ultimate root and foundation of the topic they're investigating. They assume there are multiple levels of complexity in everything, and they're eager to discover what those levels are.

The ways to become more intellectually curious might seem obvious at first glance but need to be kept uppermost in mind. If a topic rouses your interest, follow it relentlessly through reading, research, and answering your own questions. Engage with people in the field you're most interested in, and never be afraid of asking a dumb question. Embrace your state of not knowing as a launching pad, not a handicap.

Security expert George Treverton suggests that a good way to approach the unknown is as a "mystery" as opposed to a "puzzle" like a crossword or jigsaw. "Puzzles may be more satisfying, but the world increasingly offers us mysteries," Treverton wrote in *Smithsonian* magazine. "Treating them as puzzles is like trying to solve the unsolvable—an impossible challenge. But approaching them as mysteries may make us more comfortable with the uncertainties of our age."

Intellectual curiosity is not exactly the same as, say, Googling for Hollywood gossip and getting the complete story on a given Real Housewife. Instead, it's a directed effort to gain insight on a topic with relevance that resounds in our lives in some way. Author Philip Dow suggests taking 10 minutes a day—an almost ridiculously easy time commitment—to dive into a topic or subject that interests you but you haven't had the time to learn about yet.

It's even better to find a topic that has a direct impact on or a particular significance to your life—if you're a parent, you might examine child development; if you're politically active, you might study history and current issues; if you're an athlete, you might learn about motivational techniques or sports law. Whatever your choice, never be satisfied with the first answer you get: go deeper, get multiple sides, and challenge what you think you know. There's everything to gain from the intellectually curious mindset.

Remember, how differently would you act if ego and pride weren't in your way and you weren't concerned with appearing stupid or weird? You'd feel absolute freedom to pursue your curiosities down deep rabbit holes.

The Echo Chamber

Speaking of challenging what you think you know, there's a phenomenon that's snared a good portion of the population roughly since the dawn of the new millennium, especially those with rather strident and unshakeable belief systems. It's the echo chamber. This runs counter to the intellectually curious mindset, in which the most important part of learning is learning from people outside your immediate comfort or knowledge zone.

The echo chamber is a closed-off precept in which humans of all stripes and kinds tend to circulate in packs whose beliefs match their own. Rather than reach out to hear alternative or opposing viewpoints, they seek to find more "information" that supports their own opinions or standards. In reality, they only end up hearing echoes of their own viewpoints and opinions. This kind of mindset is called *"confirmation bias."*

Confirmation bias leads someone to seek out and legitimize "proof" that confirms the beliefs and theories we already espouse—and to shut out, declaim, and often berate evidence that disproves our beliefs. You see this quite frequently in current political discourse, which often leads to the acceptance of "fake news" that validates our own views. If you want to find evidence that smoking is healthy, all you need to do is type "smoking is healthy" into a search engine and you'll have found your echo chamber.

But it also occurs on more personal levels. If you've decided that a casual acquaintance is a philanderer, you might ignore testimony about their committed relationship and believe that friend of a friend who might have seen them possibly hook up with someone else from a distance.

The confirmation bias mindset can lead to far more than just intellectual rot; we've seen it damage relationships and long-time friendships. Avoiding confirmation bias and seeking to challenge your own beliefs is akin to the humbleness that one needs to learn, which takes a drastically different approach than merely finding only people to agree with. It's tough and truly requires being open to the fact that you might need to humble yourself.

One method in doing that is to take a certain belief or inclination that you have and to come up with *two* different hypotheses that differ from it—so you have three different theories to work with. Not only do you want your original belief and its theoretical opposite, but you also want a *third* explanation that might float between the two extremes or occupy a certain gray area that neither extreme necessarily considers. Seek out opposing perspectives or something that will prove the opposite of your assumptions or views. Collect as much information as you can, and make sure you're learning instead of confirming your biases and subconsciously seeking out your own echo chamber.

Then go to town and research your beliefs, finding evidence or explanations that support all three hypotheses. There's a good chance you might find yourself slightly updating or revising your original theory—and that's a *win*. It reflects your ability to understand from all sides, and you'll find out which of your core beliefs are the most important.

As an example, I'm going to try and pick a "controversial" topic that's so ridiculous it will make nobody upset: let's say you have a firmly held belief that the Abominable Snowman actually exists and is causing trouble for dwellers in the Himalayas. That's your one hypothesis.

Coming up with an opposing hypothesis should be pretty simple. The Abominable Snowman does *not* exist, and Himalayans are doing just fine. A third theory might be trickier, but it could be that the Abominable Snowman didn't quite exist as we knew him: he was in fact an extremely tall, antisocial, and hairy man that most of the Himalayans didn't like.

The first thing I'd do is find as neutral of a source as possible to find what we definitely know about the Abominable Snowman. I no doubt would have plenty of sources confirming my beliefs (websites, sympathetic friends), so I would go to them to find statements that support my own view.

Then—and this is where we all experience discomfort—I would seek out information from sources who diametrically *oppose* my point of view (other websites, friends who tell the truth, most mountaineering experts) and try to summarize their viewpoints. I'd then try to find information supporting my third hypotheses.

It's likely I would find enough information to at least revise my opinion of the Abominable Snowman's existence or change it altogether. I would take a note of that. (Once again, I urge you to come up with an actual belief or controversy that's not this unbelievable. Also, I apologize to any hardcore Abominable Snowman believers.)

This approach to tackling confirmation bias is supportive of another extraordinarily helpful mindset to cultivate: the humble, inquisitive mindset.

Humility is often confused for weakness of character, whereas qualities like presumptuousness, arrogance, pretension, and closed-mindedness are considered outward signs of inner strength.

This is possibly the biggest fallacy of philosophy in the present world—the truth is the exact opposite. Humility and curiosity show strength of character and the self-confidence to investigate the world and not be shaken down by new understandings or beliefs. In contrast, people who exhibit arrogance and narrowness almost always do so out of insecurity—they're covering up something that makes them very, very vulnerable.

Intellectual curiosity suffers under the delusion of arrogance. While the humility mindset offers access to deeper understanding and gained knowledge, the opposite mindset courts failure because the need to be "right"—or not even that, but just to be *"certain"*—is a need of the ego. The ego cares only about insularity and protection. It cares not one whit for learning, which in turn has nothing to do with ego (because you know nothing, remember?). Intellectual curiosity leads to learning, even if it's not the kind of answer you were expecting to find. The egotistical approach leads to failure because of the arrogant "need" to be correct.

The point of the humility mindset is to check your pride during the course of learning. You don't have to chuck all of it out the door at other times (though it probably wouldn't hurt), but at least in the act of finding new things, listening to others, and discovering new truths, set your pride aside.

Confronting our own beliefs isn't easy because we fear the prospect that we've lived under false impressions for most of our lives. Adopting the always-learning mindset relieves a good deal of that fear—and makes eliminating confirmation bias more of an opportunity than a risk.

You're Never There: Perpetual Progress vs. Achievement

Finally, here's some stone-cold truth that will bug some of you but hopefully relieve most of you: you are a work in progress and always will be. You will experience monumental changes in the way you think, feel, and behave over long periods of time. Most of these will be improvements and developments on your way to becoming an amazing human being. But you will, unfortunately, never *quite* be there—at least in mindset.

It's not that you won't accomplish great things or shouldn't show some pride in your achievements. It's just that you *can't stop* there. Albert Einstein published his theory of general relativity—arguably the most significant scientific moment of the 20th century—in 1915. He could have stopped right there and cemented his legacy forever. But he continued to refine his theory throughout the next decade and a half, incorporating information about electromagnetism and finally updating his findings with the theory of distant parallelism in 1929. Only when he felt he was finished did he move on to other theories.

Our actions are highly susceptible to the labels we give ourselves—the short and terse descriptors that we use to identify who we are. This is especially true with negative identifications: "lazy," "stupid," "weak," "unstable," "angry," or "unimportant."

That's why I suggest a change in your mindset of self-identification: the elimination of the phrase "*I am*" and the adoption of the phrase "*I'm working on it.*"

When you say "I am," you're immediately giving yourself a label that frankly acts more like a stamp: "I am lazy," "I am stupid," and so on. You've crystallized that belief and made it part of you. That makes change so much harder. If you really *are* lazy, the "I am" statement has boxed you in that corner and branded itself to you.

But changing that statement to reflect what you want to *become*, you've flipped the momentum. Instead of saying "I'm lazy," say "*I'm working on* being more industrious and productive." Instead of saying "I'm stupid," say "*I'm working on* improving my knowledge and study skills." Instead of saying "I'm unstable," say "*I'm working on* knowing my triggers and how to react more evenly."

Even if you're completely broke, don't say "I'm broke"—say "*I'm working on* managing my finances and finding ways to earn income." Will some people think that's just a roundabout way of saying "I'm broke"? Probably. But that's *their* label, not yours. They're just being judgmental—or I should say, "*They're working on* being more empathetic and accepting of people in challenging circumstances."

This way of thinking also keeps you in line with the humility aspect of the learning mindset if you flip it toward your positive traits. Instead of saying "I'm smart," try saying "*I'm working* on being smart." Instead of saying "I'm talented," say "*I'm working* on developing my talents." You're not saying you're *not* smart or talented. You're saying you're working on improving yourself—which can and should be an unending process. In turn, it might increase your enthusiasm for learning and discovering new things rather than stunting your enthusiasm with the idea that you already know it all.

Not only are you removing the disparaging quality from your identity, but you're also articulating your purpose every time you say you're working on something. And you'll always be working on it—because we never stop learning. Adopting the humble mindset is the best way to accept that fact and make learning and development happen more easily.

Takeaways:

- The mindset of humility is more geared toward a mindset of perpetual learning, but the latter can't happen without the former. In order to learn effectively, you must remove your ego from the equation and embrace the fact that you might not know everything and have to humble yourself.

- You can do this first by trying to use the beginner's mindset. This is when you attempt to act as if you are seeing things for the first time. When something is novel, you are completely open to information. What questions might you ask and what details might you focus on? Step out of your expert mindset of seeing the big picture only and get back to a beginner's curiosity.

- Intellectual curiosity also helps because it encourages you to simply pursue knowledge and dig below the surface level of information you are bound to find. View people as sources of complex, fascinating knowledge and seek to discover it for your own benefit. To lower your guard enough to properly learn, you also need to learn to avoid the echo chamber, which is where your opinions and viewpoints get amplified. Instead, you need to get into the habit of seeking out opposing and alternative viewpoints to avoid confirmation bias.

- The final aspect of humility is to tell yourself that you are never quite at your destination. This isn't to lower your self-esteem; rather, it's to put you into the mode of constant learning and always striving for more, as opposed to being satisfied with adequacy. We are all unfinished products; at least view yourself that way in order to feel that continual learning and progress is necessary.

Chapter 8. The Mindset of the Present

John is only sixteen years old, but he feels the weight of the world on his shoulders.

His parents, teachers, and guidance counselor are pushing him to plan one of the most important decisions of his life, his career, right now. He doesn't know what job will make him happy. He doesn't know how much money he needs to earn. He's never even managed a budget! He spends hours ruminating and poring over advice columns and college websites, but nothing seems to help. He's positive that he needs to go to college, but for what?

Should he take a risk on a more interesting but lower-paying career, or should he choose a path with better pay and more job security? Would he be happy if he chose the latter option? What if he chose the former option, and the lower pay left him desperate? What if a good school wouldn't even accept him; would that mar his chances for life?

He's worried—very worried—and not much is helping his anxiety. He spends so much time worrying about his future, trying to figure out the rest of his life, that he starts losing his grasp on what's happening around him. He's stopped talking to most of his friends, and he rarely accepts invitations anymore. Instead, he spends his time reading and worrying, worrying and reading. Soon his anxiety would interfere with his sleep and distract him while studying, lowering his grades and genuinely limiting his chances of attaining his own best future.

Because John can't stop fretting about the future, he's losing his friends, his sanity, and his future.

His mother, Julia, has the opposite problem. When she looks at her current life, she sees little of interest. Feeling empty, she retreats into her mind, relishing the hope and excitement of her high school days. Sure, the work was hard, but overcoming academic challenges was a fulfilling struggle that afforded her the opportunity to triumph. She still wishes she'd spent more time on her studies. Back then, her main priority was maintaining her friendships. She'd stay out late, gossiping and laughing for hours with her friends.

She can't remember the last time she went out with friends. It had to have been years ago. As a stay-at-home mom, her family has become the sum total of her life. Often, she thinks about how different her life could've been if she'd finished her college degree instead of dropping out to get married and become a mother. At the time, it had seemed like a good idea.

She was deeply in love and eager to have kids. Her husband and children still make her happy, but it isn't enough. She wishes she hadn't thrown away all those opportunities. She could have been self-reliant and respected. She could have made a real difference in the world. But now she's a middle-aged parent with a decades' wide gap in her resume. What could she do now?

Career-wise, she was finished. She's made her choices; there's nothing she can do. Julia is so preoccupied with her past decisions and the life she used to live that she hardly notices the joy abounding in her current life. Her nostalgia even prevents her from seeing the opportunities she currently has to improve herself and her life. Being stuck in the past is making her miserable in the present.

Both mother and son have great intentions; it's good to plan our futures, and it's equally good to reflect upon our past. That's how we learn and choose what to do with ourselves. But both went wrong by being so focused on their thoughts that they lost track of the circumstances, responsibilities, and opportunities right in front of them.

Focusing on that would let them make the most of their lives.

Author Eckhart Tolle has great insight into the problem of fixating on the past or future; he once said, "All negativity is caused by an accumulation of psychological time and denial of the present. Unease, anxiety, tension, stress, worry—all forms of fear—are caused by too much *future* and not enough presence. Guilt, regret, resentment, grievances, sadness, bitterness, and all forms of non-forgiveness are caused by too much *past*, and not enough presence."

Tolle claims that focusing on the future causes fear that manifests as unease, anxiety, tension, stress, and worry. In other words, fears about what could happen stress us out. Thinking about the future to solve problems turns bad when fear becomes stronger than hope. Fear becomes a problem when, for whatever reason, we can't easily find a satisfying conclusion.

In an ideal world, we would admit that we can't predict or control things and wait to see what happens. But instead, we worry. And worrying produces stress, which releases cortisone and adrenaline into our bodies, leading to higher levels of baseline anxiety and the tight, stiff muscles that come with it. The real pickle is that when we feel bad mentally and physically, like we do when we're stressed, it becomes even harder to solve our problems. This amplifies our stress and our worries, leading to a vicious, self-destructive cycle that keeps us firmly fixated on the future and the horrible outcomes we fear.

Conversely, when we fixate on our failures, whether it's insulting a kid in second grade, failing our driver's test, or a real mistake, like committing a felony, we are failing to forgive ourselves. We are focusing on what we did in the past, on the people we used to be, rather than on who and what we are now. People learn from their mistakes. Improving over time is a good thing, and we can't do that unless we mess up first. But too often, we identify with our guilt and shame; we think our worst decisions define our character.

The past, along with everything we've done, is gone. It can't be changed; it can only be accepted. We cannot allow it to linger, dominating our lives and moods with negativity.

Forgiving ourselves, others, and the world is essential, but Tolle mentions another ingredient for avoiding the negative emotions that erupt when we're immersed in the wrong time: presence. Forgiveness allows us to focus on the present more easily, but what other steps can we take to be more present?

Moving Beyond the Past

Contemplating our mishaps has a certain allure. Unlike present actions, the outcomes of which we can't yet know, the past is resolved. We know the outcome of each action; we've lived through it. We know the emotions and consequences that erupted from our decisions, and we can no longer do anything to fix those mistakes.

This powerlessness can feel liberating because it frees us of the responsibility to act.

We've already made our choice, it's said and done, and relief comes with that sense of finality. If nothing else, it's a stark and comforting contrast to the uncertainty of the future. In a way, it's safer to ponder mistakes and wonder what could have happened if we'd acted differently than to make a decision and act in the present, when more failure may lurk around the bend.

But lingering on the past is a massive waste of time and energy because the present is all we have. We don't live in the past or the future, but in the now. We can't take paths we missed in the past, and we can't know what our current choices will bring until our futures become our present. We can only try our best and make the smartest decisions we can. Anything else is impossible, and holding anyone to impossible standards only invites regret, anger, bitterness, resentment, and hatred—

of yourself, other people, and the hand of fate alike.

The first step toward breaking this destructive habit is asking yourself why you're stuck in the past. What emotion is making you return to the past? Do you feel guilty about something you did? Do you regret something you didn't do? Are you resentful about old wounds? Are you bitter that opportunities were taken from you? Pinpoint your grievance, accept that it can't be changed, and forgive everyone—including yourself—for being imperfect.

People make mistakes. While mistakes are frustrating, their existence is inevitable. Often, they're even helpful. Think about it: do you remember the right answers you had on the tests you took in school? Odds are, you don't. You were told you knew what you were doing, so you didn't linger on it. But mistakes stand out. We see that red ink, and we're bothered that we did poorly. This distress encourages us to review the material we missed, and the added weight of having been wrong solidifies the message in our minds. Because we made mistakes, we remember the true answers, the better actions, and the more compassionate approaches more readily. So being wrong is good. If we're willing to learn our lessons, it helps us become better, more successful people.

But what about when people choose to hurt us? We learn from that, too. We can learn to identify and avoid hurtful people and situations from poor experiences in the past. A woman is unlikely to walk back into a particular bar after being pawed like a cat toy by men in that locale, for example. That's a lesson learned. Most of the times that we're wronged can supply us with similar lessons, making us stronger and wiser as we collect life experience.

Bad things happen to everyone, but focusing on being a victim gives all your agency to the past. By contrast, seeing yourself as a fighter or a survivor roots you in the present.

Fighters actively confront their pain, learn from it, resolve lingering emotions, and work toward forgiveness and acceptance. Survivors have finished that work and put their experiences behind them. They know they went through hard times, but they emerged on the other side. They understand that they're stronger, wiser, and more experienced than people who haven't seen those aspects of our world. Neither fighters nor survivors stand down and accept their past defining their present. Instead, they leave it behind and focus on the change they're creating right now.

What's happening right now, for you, in the present moment? You're reading, but where are you? Is it comfortable? Are you hungry or thirsty, and do you have the means to fix it? Are you tired or ill and able to rest soon? What else is going on around you right this second? No matter where you are, it's probably nothing terrible. Most of us live calm, peaceful lives that contain innumerable reasons to be happy. As humans, we're prone to lingering on the few bad moments in every day and getting stuck on errors and disappointments we experienced, but the present moment? That's usually pretty good. We all need to notice that, to appreciate that, more often.

Accepting an Uncertain Future

Anticipating and planning for our future needs is often extolled as a virtue in society, and it's definitely important for us to act in ways that will make our lives easier in later years. For example, when we don't save for retirement, we find ourselves scrambling in desperation when we become too old to perform our jobs adequately. Similarly, investing in our future housing stability by buying a house or our future career options by taking skill-development courses is not only wise but often necessary. When we perform these actions, we are creating a more stable, secure, and comfortable life for our future selves. But even this version of living for the future, commendable as it is, can be overdone.

Consider the case of the diligent young man who lives well below his means, siphons almost all his income into savings and investments, and is hit by a bus at 34. He couldn't have known he was wasting his life—he was doing the "right" thing—but he never got to enjoy the fruits of his labor. His hard work was in vain.

Tomorrow can't be taken for granted by any of us, nor can reaching a ripe old age. Saving is important. Acting to ensure our lasting well-being is indispensable. But delaying all or most of our happiness for the sake of a future that may never come sacrifices the present for the future and drains happiness from life. Balance is necessary. Plan and act *for* the future but live and act *in* the moment.

Imagining our future can help us crystallize our goals and enhance our confidence if we do it in moderation, but goals are only useful when they are followed by real, daily action. When dreams of the future distract us from performing those tasks, they're a waste of time at best. At worst, they're creating dread and despair for our current lives because we aren't living the life we want.

When we do this, we've raised our expectations so high that all we feel is disappointment. Worse, this mismatch between our expectations and what we feel we deserve can quickly lead to anxiety. Will we ever get what we want? Will we ever be good enough? How can anyone make that much progress? These anxious trains of thought can further propel people toward daydreaming, as it makes daily life more and more unpleasant. Avoid this by setting reasonable, achievable, stepwise goals for yourself. When you see yourself getting closer to your goals, it's easy to imagine reaching your final destination.

Keeping our brains too fixated on the future damages our happiness, even when we have modest expectations, if we allow our anxiety to take over. It's easy to be afraid that people will boo us off the stage during a speech or that our car will break down on a long drive. It's even easier to imagine the hundred ways that we can fail ourselves by not having the strength or character needed to do our work.

But in reality, most people are kind and will accept gaffes, mistakes, or even the occasional calamity. In reality, the world isn't out to get us; it's filled with kind people who are willing to help and a million opportunities that most of us can't imagine until we see them before us. And in reality, most of the things that can go wrong won't go wrong. Wasting our time fretting for hours, days, or years over mistakes and misfortunes that will, in most cases, not happen is needless.

Worries are only useful as a reminder. If you're worried you're going to mess up your speech, stop thinking about it and practice more instead. If you're worried about your car breaking down, make sure to carry your cell phone and sign up for a roadside assistance service. If there is something you can do to prevent misfortunes, do that thing, then let the worry go. You've done your best.

Meanwhile, if you're anxious about something that you can't control or mitigate, there's no benefit in worrying at all; you're better off enjoying life or working to improve your world. After all, it's not like worrying about a potential problem makes that problem any less likely; it only makes you devote more of your life to that event than necessary—and at a critical cost.

Worrying activates the body's stress response, increasing blood pressure, cortisol levels, and the amount of adrenaline pumping through our veins. Combined, these contribute to heart disease, weight gain, insomnia, and some truly unpleasant neurological changes; the effects of these outcomes range from death to improving your likelihood of making poor decisions in the future.

How do we avoid this? Relax a little. Be kind to yourself. Remind yourself that what you "should" do is no more important than what you "want" to do. Treat yourself when you can afford the expense, calories, and lost time. Remember that plans can change and mistakes are not the end of the world. Get enough sleep. Set time aside in each day to enjoy the little things. Without this focus on your present needs, your present life, it's easy to run yourself into the ground and burn out before you even come close to the life you want to live. Go slow and steady; that's the only way to win.

Just don't take it too far. Forgetting the future entirely will make you forget to strive for better things. Similarly, avoiding thoughts of tomorrow can be a way to avoid facing the inevitable change of life. You, your life, your capacities, and your possessions will not remain constant from birth to death. Bodies and minds grow old, people move on, and physical objects break and deteriorate. We must learn to minimize these damages and maximize our gains despite these potentially frustrating facts of life. Giving a thoughtful eye to the future, figuring out a good plan of action, and enacting that plan in our present is the way through. Identify what you need to do and act instead of letting fear develop.

How to Live in the Present

How can we stay in the present? How can we develop our ability to remain conscious of our current environment and actions? Better yet, how can we pull ourselves back to the present when we get stuck lingering on our futures and pasts?

Focus on the present moment. Notice the interactions and processes occurring around you. Quietly observe actions as they unfold and notice your place in the times and locations you experience. Consider any thoughts that arise, but don't linger on them. The point of this exercise is to really notice the world outside of you and how you can shape and change it with your body and mind. This is great to do while baking or performing housework and can transform the experience from an unpleasant task you can't wait to finish into a fascinating exploration of the world we occupy.

Pay attention to your senses while going about your day. When you smell something, consider what you can hear or see at the same time. Notice the feeling of fabric on your skin and the breeze through your hair as you move. Feel sunshine, smell the grass and the flowers you pass, and really notice the complex and nuanced flavors of your food. When we focus on our senses, instead of dismissing the information they offer us, a wealth of riches can be discovered in the most mundane events. It also helps us stay connected to our environment, which keeps us in the moment.

Pay attention to your body. Consider and correct your posture. Scan your body to find areas of tension, then tighten and relax those muscles to relieve stress. Pay attention when you feel hungry or thirsty rather than immediately grabbing some food or drink. Notice whether what you really feel is hunger, boredom, or a need for emotional fulfillment; act accordingly. When we genuinely notice what we feel physically, we become more grounded and less prone to distraction.

Learn to meditate and make it a regular practice. The easiest way to start out is through a simple breathing exercise. Breathe in, noticing the physical sensations of your lungs filling with air. Then breathe out while noticing all of the details of that sensation. The important thing here, as in a lot of meditative practices, is to focus on one thing for an extended period of time. Anything can be a focus of simple, singular contemplation like this, but focusing on breathing is one of the easier ways to start.

However you decide to meditate, know that you will be distracted. Thoughts will arise in your mind. When they do, notice them for what they are and return to the object you're focusing on. Over time, it will become easier to let go of thoughts and focus on a chosen object. Once you gain that discipline, it's a lot easier to dismiss anxious or distracting thoughts in your day-to-day life.

Allow yourself unspeakable, childlike joy. Children explore the world in a simple, naïve, and hopeful manner. They play with toys, make up games, and form attachments with gusto. Reviving some of your childlike fervor by allowing yourself to experience that same joy as an adult can amp up your ability to live without fear, and that's a great way to stay in the present moment.

Write down things you're happy about or grateful for every day. If you make this a consistent practice, you'll find more and more reasons to be glad every day. Often, we take for granted the good things in life, leaving us with painful and unfortunate events to focus on. Forming a habit of noticing the good trains us out of that mindset and makes us appreciate all the good stuff that happens every day. Even better, writing down the details gives us an easy reference sheet to remind us of all the good things that have happened and will happen to us again in the future. It's a lot harder to be carried away by negative thoughts when you have proof of all the good in your life!

When you're getting stuff done, monotask, don't multitask. Monotasking has been shown to increase focus, happiness, and the quality of our work while reducing stress. All of these help our days go smoothly and our goals get accomplished; that makes it easier to appreciate our current lives.

Take small steps toward the life you want. Often, it can feel like our endgame is a million miles away and we'll never reach it. That can make us discouraged, encouraging us to give up. But almost every goal affords us something that can be done to get closer to it, even if it's as small as reading an article or setting up a savings account. Small steps, when put together, allow for a lot of progress. If you work toward your goals for twenty or thirty minutes every day, you'll be who you want to be, doing exactly what you want to do, in no time at all.

Release tension, set intention. This tip comes from the book *High Performance Habits* by Brendon Burchard. To do it, stop between projects or events in your life to take two to three minutes to focus on your breathing, releasing all the tension from your body. Our prior steps about meditating and focusing on your body should help. After you do this, think about how you want to move forward right now. When you do this, you'll find that the tasks you perform in a day transform from an endless series of events to complete into isolated tasks that are approached with singular focus. This will increase your performance by keeping your current task in the forefront of your mind.

When you notice your thoughts drifting unconsciously to the past or future—and you will; we all do—take that drifting as a cue that you need to perform one or more of the focusing tasks listed above. You don't have to give in to the cycle; the distracted thoughts themselves can be your cue to dive right back into the present moment.

Remember, our whole lives exist in the now, and our actions in those successive moments are what we should be thinking about most of the time. That way we notice all the calm, peaceful, joyful things we encounter, and we remember to stay calmly and dutifully on the path that will lead us to our goals.

When we think of the past, it should be to learn a lesson, resolve emotions, or relive a pleasant experience. If we spiral into unpleasantness, we need to engage in actions that will pull us back to the peace and joy of the present moment. Similarly, when we think of the future, it should always be with an eye toward inspiring our current actions and planning our path to our goals. If it isn't directly informing or motivating current actions, it's taking up time for no purpose and we must recall ourselves to the current time. In the end, we can only control the present moment. The past is gone, the future is uncertain, but the life we're living right here, right now? That's real. We control that. Let's make it good.

Takeaways:

- Stay present. It's something we hear frequently, but what does it mean? Simply put, we are more often caught in the past or looking forward to the future. When we are caught in the past, we are affected by things and events that we

have no control over. When we are looking forward to the future (excessively, of course), we are also affected by that which we have no control over.
- Author Eckhart Tolle has great insight into the problem of fixating on the past or future; he once said, "All negativity is caused by an accumulation of psychological time and denial of the present. Unease, anxiety, tension, stress, worry—all forms of fear—are caused by too much *future* and not enough presence. Guilt, regret, resentment, grievances, sadness, bitterness, and all forms of non-forgiveness are caused by too much *past*, and not enough presence."
- To let go of the past is to forgive, excuse, and allow for errors. We can learn from the past, and we don't have to experience things in vain. To stop fixating on the future is to accept uncertainty and a certain amount of randomness. We cannot control very much in our lives, and all we can control is our actions and reactions.

- Staying in the present is of course easier said than done, but the practice of meditation is a useful blueprint. It is important to clear your mind and simply lose yourself in a thought, feeling, or sensation. Preoccupation is the worst of sins here, and it can only be defeated with time and practice—and the knowledge that the past does not matter anymore and the future is out of our control.

Summary Guide

Chapter 1. Mind Over Matter

- What is your mindset? It's how you see the world, yourself, and your place in the world. It's the overall lens you view everything through. It includes your self-talk, your internal voice, and the narrative or story you tell yourself *about* yourself. It's not technically hard to change because there is no physical activity involved, but it's hard because effort doesn't always correlate to results. Simply thinking different can be one of the toughest tasks in the world.

- Mindset has the power to shape your reality, as proven by the concept of the self-fulfilling prophecy. Famous instances of this include Oedipus and Clever Hans, a horse who appeared to be able to do arithmetic and read. This, along with the placebo effect, wherein a belief or expectation makes that belief or expectation exist, are stunning illustrations of how powerful your mind can be. It's not just positive thinking; it's thinking strategically about what you want and what you don't want. In a sense, your mindset should enable you to put mind over matter or simply overpower your circumstances through your beliefs alone.

Chapter 2. The Mindset of Agency and Control

- It's easy to feel like you aren't in control of your life. After all, we literally aren't in control of anyone's actions but our own. But we must not take the easy way out by giving up control completely to externalities and other people's whims. We ultimately become powerless because we believe it.

- The first way this tends to happen is through adopting a fixed mindset. A fixed mindset is where you feel that your abilities and possibilities are fixed and limited, whereas a growth mindset accurately states that you are limited only by your efforts and actions. If you have a fixed mindset, you don't feel that things can change, so why attempt to change? A growth mindset lends itself to growth and development, knowing that effort and hard work is the catalyst.

- The second way we tend to feel powerless is through unwittingly having an external locus of control. This is when you feel that your life is fully determined by things external to you—other people, circumstances, and luck. We feel that things are predetermined and a matter of fate. This stands in contrast to an internal locus of control, where you feel that you have the power to impact your life in whatever way you wish—within reason. Again, the latter is far more associated with success because it pushes you toward achievement.

- The third and final way we might feel that we lack agency in our own lives is through adopting a helpless mindset versus a self-efficacious mindset. The former is a learned behavior that nothing will change even if you act, so therefore, you stop acting. It may have been the case once or twice, but generally, an input creates an outcome. The self-efficacious mindset is a belief in one's own abilities. This belief can be grown through personal experiences, affirmations from others, vicarious experiences, and emotional and physiological states.

Chapter 3. The Mindset of Perseverance

- Perseverance is one of the keys to what we want in life. Life is tough, so we ultimately need to develop or find helmets to get to where we want. We can't hope to get through life planning for the absence of hardship; rather, we must plan for it and plan for what to do once it happens.

- One of the best tools you can have to build mental toughness is Stoicism, a centuries-old life philosophy that is all about consciously and intentionally choosing your thoughts. The reality is that all of life's events, even the ones that we find joy in, are neutral. We are only emotionally affected because we choose to assign judgment and perspective to them. Thus, we can select to view hardship as a learning experience, and we can also train ourselves to not react through negative visualization and practicing voluntary discomfort. Finally, we must realize that there is very little in this world that we can control. Thus, all we can do is try our best and accept what comes.

- In gaining perseverance and mental toughness, we must also understand what impacts us and what does not. We are very frequently suckered into feeling urgent and immediate anxiety about negative events. But when you zoom out onto a long enough timeline, we will all die and disappear from the earth. Does this lessen the impact of daily annoyances and setbacks?

- Finally, the 40% rule as popularized by Navy SEALs is instructive to redefining our limitations. In essence, when we think we've reached our limits, we have probably reached only about 40%—not even a majority percentage. We will suffer and feel discomfort, but we will not break. We may bend, but we will still be able to get up after being knocked down. Thus, the final portion of perseverance is to expect pain and only be pleasantly surprised when it is less than you expected.

Chapter 4. The Mindset of Action

- We all know we should think more. But there comes a certain point in which action is necessary. This seems counterintuitive, but studies have shown that thinking and doing are mutually exclusive. Therefore, in order to get from Point A to Point B, action is necessary, even if the steps are small and seemingly useless. You'll also have to force yourself to stop learning and consuming information to take action, but in the end, it works out better because the best way of gathering information is firsthand experience.

- You must be mindful to avoid the problem-oriented mindset; instead, strive for the solution-oriented mindset. The former simply asks why in the face of an obstacle while the latter asks, "What now?" when faced with the same. One spurs action while the other is caught in emotional meandering and fixation. Solutions are a clear point of action while problems are a refusal to move forward.

- Finally, we often confuse what it actually takes to get us feeling good about action. To be specific, most of us feel that we are seeking out motivation that creates action. But this is wrong and, in fact, in reverse. We will never be able to find a compelling reason or motivation to do things; it is unreliable at best and nonexistent at worst. So we should be using action itself to create momentum and then motivation.

Chapter 5. The Mindset of Belief

- The mindset of thinking big is where you attempt to completely bypass your limiting beliefs. When you dare to think big and dream, you may find that you achieve much more simply by planning for it. One way to do this is by thinking in terms of BHAGs—big, hairy, audacious goals. Instead of shooting for X, shoot for 10X and rethink exactly what's possible and necessary.

- Thinking big, however, does not stand alone, and that's where systems thinking comes in. Think in terms of a system instead of a goal; a system is merely a series of consistent tasks, whereas a goal is a one-time occurrence or achievement. Focus on the small actions that the system dictates and you will find yourself closer to your goals as a matter of circumstance.

- Finally, an alter ego has the surprising power of completely changing your perceptions and beliefs. That's because it's not you. Your alter ego, to be most effective, should represent your ideal self. What do you wish you were more or less of? What traits are you seeking? What beliefs do you want to embody?

That's what your alter ego should epitomize because you already know what *you'll* do in certain situations and it's something you want to change. Conveniently, the alter ego also serves as a buffer to our sense of ego and pride.

Chapter 6. The Mindset of Gratitude

- It is virtually impossible to be grateful and unhappy at the same time. Seek to inject this type of happiness into your daily life. Bad things happen every day, and yet some people are more resilient. This is because of gratitude and the power it has to eliminate negative thoughts.

- Gratitude has been shown to create a host of physical and psychological benefits. Those aren't important; rather, it's more important to understand how to show daily gratitude. You can do this by complimenting others, seeking perspective, asking what you can learn from setbacks or failures, and making a commitment to not complain or give voice to your negative thoughts.

- Optimism, even if you have to force it at first, has also shown a host of benefits. Smiling can literally change your body's chemistry, and everything else about optimism can best be summed up as cultivating the habit of looking at the bright side of things. To stay positive, optimistic, and grateful, cut out negative people from your life, understand that life is a marathon, pay attention to your changes and improvements, and try to embrace a solution-oriented approach.

Chapter 7. The Mindset of Humility

- The mindset of humility is more geared toward a mindset of perpetual learning, but the latter can't happen without the former. In order to learn effectively, you must remove your ego from the equation and embrace the fact that you might not know everything and have to humble yourself.

- You can do this first by trying to use the beginner's mindset. This is when you attempt to act as if you are seeing things for the first time. When something is novel, you are completely open to information. What questions might you ask and what details might you focus on? Step out of your expert mindset of seeing the big picture only and get back to a beginner's curiosity.

- Intellectual curiosity also helps because it encourages you to simply pursue knowledge and dig below the surface level of information you are bound to find. View people as sources of complex, fascinating knowledge and seek to discover it for your own benefit. To lower your guard enough to properly learn, you also need to learn to avoid the echo chamber, which is where your opinions and viewpoints get amplified. Instead, you need to get into the habit of seeking out opposing and alternative viewpoints to avoid confirmation bias.

- The final aspect of humility is to tell yourself that you are never quite at your destination. This isn't to lower your self-esteem; rather, it's to put you into the mode of constant learning and always striving for more, as opposed to being satisfied with adequacy. We are all unfinished products; at least view yourself that way in order to feel that continual learning and progress is necessary.

Chapter 8. The Mindset of the Present

- Stay present. It's something we hear frequently, but what does it mean? Simply put, we are more often caught in the past or looking forward to the future. When we are caught in the past, we are affected by things and events that we have no control over. When we are looking forward to the future (excessively, of course), we are also affected by that which we have no control over.
- Author Eckhart Tolle has great insight into the problem of fixating on the past or future; he once said, "All negativity is caused by an accumulation of psychological time and denial of the present. Unease, anxiety, tension, stress, worry—all forms of fear—are caused by too much *future* and not enough presence. Guilt, regret, resentment,

grievances, sadness, bitterness, and all forms of non-forgiveness are caused by too much *past*, and not enough presence."
- To let go of the past is to forgive, excuse, and allow for errors. We can learn from the past, and we don't have to experience things in vain. To stop fixating on the future is to accept uncertainty and a certain amount of randomness. We cannot control very much in our lives, and all we can control is our actions and reactions.
- Staying in the present is of course easier said than done, but the practice of meditation is a useful blueprint. It is important to clear your mind and simply lose yourself in a thought, feeling, or sensation. Preoccupation is the worst of sins here, and it can only be defeated with time and practice—and the knowledge that the past does not matter anymore and the future is out of our control.

www.ingramcontent.com/pod-product-compliance
Lightning Source LLC
Chambersburg PA
CBHW071157070526
44584CB00019B/2822